Reader's Digest

Soups & Casseroles

Published by The Reader's Digest Association Limited
London • New York • Sydney • Montreal

Soups and Casseroles is part of a series of cookery books called
Eat Well Live Well and was created by Amazon Publishing Limited.

Series Editor *Norma MacMillan*
Volume Editor *Bridget Jones*
Art Director *Ruth Prentice*
Photographic Direction *Ruth Prentice*
DTP *Peter Howard*
Editorial Assistant *Jasmine Brown*
Nutritionist *Fiona Hunter BSc Hons (Nutri.), Dip. Dietetics*

Contributors
Writers *Sara Buenfeld, Carole Clements, Linda Collister, Gail Duff,
Beverly LeBlanc, Sara Lewis, Maggie Mayhew, Kate Moseley,
Maggie Pannell, Marlena Spieler, Susanna Tee*
Recipe Testers *Catherine Atkinson, Valerie Barrett, Anna Brandenburger,
Bridget Colvin, Emma-Lee Gow, Clare Lewis, Gina Steer, Susanna Tee*
Photographers *Martin Brigdale, Gus Filgate, Amanda Heywood,
Graham Kirk, William Lingwood, Simon Smith*
Stylists *L.J. Crompton, Penny Markham, Helen Payne, Helen Trent*
Home Economists *Caroline Barty, Maxine Clark, Lisa Heathcote,
Louise Pickford, Bridget Sargeson, Joy Skipper, Linda Tubby, Sunil Vijayakar*

For Reader's Digest
Series Editor *Christine Noble*
Editorial Assistant *Caroline Boucher*
Production Controllers *Kathy Brown, Jane Holyer*

Reader's Digest General Books
Editorial Director *Cortina Butler*
Art Director *Nick Clark*

ISBN 0 276 42796 3

First Edition Copyright © 2000
The Reader's Digest Association Limited
11 Westferry Circus, Canary Wharf, London E14 4HE

Paperback edition 2003

...East Limited
...iation Far East Limited

...roduced, stored in a retrieval
...electronic, electrostatic,
...or otherwise, without

...are registered trademarks of The
...ew York, USA.

...s and the service we
...so please feel free to
...vice@readersdigest.co.uk
...ooks, you can contact us

Notes for the reader
• Use all metric or all imperial measures when preparing a recipe, as the two sets
of measurements are not exact equivalents.
• Recipes were tested using metric measures and conventional (not fan-assisted)
ovens. Medium eggs were used, unless otherwise specified.
• Can sizes are approximate, as weights can vary slightly according to the
manufacturer.
• Preparation and cooking times are only intended as a guide.

The nutritional information in this book is for reference only.
The editors urge anyone with continuing medical problems or symptoms to
consult a doctor.

Contents

Eating well to live well

Eating a healthy diet can help you look good, feel great and have lots of energy. Nutrition fads come and go, but the simple keys to eating well remain the same: enjoy a variety of food – no single food contains all the vitamins, minerals, fibre and other essential components you need for health and vitality – and get the balance right by looking at the proportions of the different foods you eat. Add some regular exercise too – at least 30 minutes a day, 3 times a week – and you'll be helping yourself to live well and make the most of your true potential.

Getting it into proportion

Current guidelines are that most people in the UK should eat more starchy foods, more fruit and vegetables, and less fat, meat products and sugary foods. It is almost impossible to give exact amounts that you should eat, as every single person's requirements vary, depending on size, age and the amount of energy expended during the day. However, nutrition experts have suggested an ideal balance of the different foods that provide us with energy (calories) and the nutrients needed for health. The number of daily portions of each of the food groups will vary from person to person – for example, an active teenager might need to eat up to 14 portions of starchy carbohydrates every day, whereas a sedentary adult would only require 6 or 7 portions – but the proportions of the food groups in relation to each other should ideally stay the same.

More detailed explanations of food groups and nutritional terms can be found on pages 156–158, together with brief guidelines on amounts which can be used in conjunction with the nutritional analyses of the recipes. A simple way to get the balance right, however, is to imagine a daily 'plate' divided into the different food groups. On the imaginary 'plate', starchy carbohydrates fill at least one-third of the space, thus constituting the main part of your meals. Fruit and vegetables fill the same amount of space. The remaining third of the 'plate' is divided mainly between protein foods and dairy foods, with just a little space allowed for foods containing fat and sugar. These are the proportions to aim for.

It isn't essential to eat the ideal proportions on the 'plate' at every meal, or even every day – balancing them over a week or two is just as good. The healthiest diet for you and your family is one that is generally balanced and sustainable in the long term.

Our daily plate

Starchy carbohydrate foods: eat 6–14 portions a day

At least 50% of the calories in a healthy diet should come from carbohydrates, and most of that from starchy foods – bread, potatoes and other starchy vegetables, pasta, rice and cereals. For most people in the UK this means doubling current intake. Starchy carbohydrate foods are best for energy. They also provide protein and essential vitamins and minerals, particularly those from the B group. Eat a variety of starchy foods, choosing wholemeal or wholegrain types whenever possible, because the fibre they contain helps to prevent constipation, bowel disease, heart disease and other health problems.

What is a portion of starchy foods?

Some examples are: 3 tbsp breakfast cereal • 2 tbsp muesli • 1 slice of bread or toast • 1 bread roll, bap or bun • 1 small pitta bread, naan bread or chapatti • 3 crackers or crispbreads • 1 medium-sized potato • 1 medium-sized plantain or small sweet potato • 2 heaped tbsp boiled rice • 2 heaped tbsp boiled pasta.

Fruit and vegetables: eat at least 5 portions a day

Nutrition experts are unanimous that we would all benefit from eating more fruit and vegetables each day – a total of at least 400 g (14 oz) of fruit and vegetables (edible part) is the target. Fruit and vegetables provide vitamin C for immunity and healing, and other 'antioxidant' vitamins and minerals for protection against cardiovascular disease and cancer. They also offer several 'phytochemicals' that help protect against cancer, and B vitamins, especially folate, which is important for women planning a pregnancy, to prevent birth defects. All of these, plus other nutrients, work together to boost well-being.

Antioxidant nutrients (e.g. vitamins C and beta-carotene, which are mainly derived from fruit and vegetables) and vitamin E help to prevent harmful free radicals in the body initiating or accelerating cancer, heart disease, cataracts, arthritis, general ageing, sun damage to skin, and damage to sperm. Free radicals occur naturally as a by-product of normal cell function, but are also caused by pollutants such as tobacco smoke and over-exposure to sunlight.

What is a portion of fruit or vegetables?

Some examples are: 1 medium-sized portion of vegetables or salad • 1 medium-sized piece of fresh fruit • 6 tbsp (about 140 g/5 oz) stewed or canned fruit • 1 small glass (100 ml/3½ fl oz) fruit juice.

Dairy foods: eat 2–3 portions a day

Dairy foods, such as milk, cheese, yogurt and fromage frais, are the best source of calcium for strong bones and teeth, and important for the nervous system. They also provide some protein for growth and repair, vitamin B_{12}, and vitamin A for healthy eyes. They are particularly valuable foods for young children, who need full-fat versions at least up to age 2. Dairy foods are also especially important for adolescent girls to prevent the development of osteoporosis later in life, and for women throughout life generally.

To limit fat intake, wherever possible adults should choose lower-fat dairy foods, such as semi-skimmed milk and low-fat yogurt.

What is a portion of dairy foods?

Some examples are: 1 medium-sized glass (200 ml/7 fl oz) milk • 1 matchbox-sized piece (40 g/1½ oz) Cheddar cheese • 1 small pot of yogurt • 125 g (4½ oz) cottage cheese or fromage frais.

Protein foods: eat 2–4 portions a day

Lean meat, fish, eggs and vegetarian alternatives provide protein for growth and cell repair, as well as iron to prevent anaemia. Meat also provides B vitamins for healthy nerves and digestion, especially vitamin B_{12}, and zinc for growth and healthy bones and skin. Only moderate amounts of these protein-rich foods are required. An adult woman needs about 45 g of protein a day and an adult man 55 g, which constitutes about 11% of a day's calories. This is less than the current average intake. For optimum health, we need to eat some protein every day.

What is a portion of protein-rich food?

Some examples are: 3 slices (85–100 g/3–3½ oz) of roast beef, pork, ham, lamb or chicken • about 100 g (3½ oz) grilled offal • 115–140 g (4–5 oz) cooked fillet of white or oily fish (not fried in batter) • 3 fish fingers • 2 eggs (up to 7 a week) • about 140 g/5 oz baked beans • 60 g (2¼ oz) nuts, peanut butter or other nut products.

Foods containing fat 1–5 portions a day

Unlike fruit, vegetables and starchy carbohydrates, which can be eaten in abundance, fatty foods should not exceed 33% of the day's calories in a balanced diet, and only 10% of this should be from saturated fat. This quantity of fat may seem a lot, but it isn't – fat contains more than twice as many calories per gram as either carbohydrate or protein.

Overconsumption of fat is a major cause of weight and health problems. A healthy diet must contain a certain amount of fat to provide fat-soluble vitamins and essential fatty acids, needed for the development and function of the brain, eyes and nervous system, but we only need a small amount each day – just 25 g is required, which is much less than we consume in our Western diet. The current recommendations from the Department of Health are a maximum of 71 g fat (of this, 21.5 g saturated) for women each day and 93.5 g fat (28.5 g saturated) for men. The best sources of the essential fatty acids are natural fish oils and pure vegetable oils.

What is a portion of fatty foods?

Some examples are: 1 tsp butter or margarine • 2 tsp low-fat spread • 1 tsp cooking oil • 1 tbsp mayonnaise or vinaigrette (salad dressing) • 1 tbsp cream • 1 individual packet of crisps.

Foods containing sugar: 0–2 portions a day

Although many foods naturally contain sugars (e.g. fruit contains fructose, milk lactose), health experts recommend that we limit 'added' sugars. Added sugars, such as table sugar, provide only calories – they contain no vitamins, minerals or fibre to contribute to health, and it is not necessary to eat them at all. But, as the old adage goes, 'a little of what you fancy does you good' and sugar is no exception. Denial of foods, or using them as rewards or punishment, is not a healthy attitude to eating, and can lead to cravings, binges and yo-yo dieting. Sweet foods are a pleasurable part of a well-balanced diet, but added sugars should account for no more than 11% of the total daily carbohydrate intake.

In assessing how much sugar you consume, don't forget that it is a major ingredient of many processed and ready-prepared foods.

What is a portion of sugary foods?

Some examples are: 3 tsp sugar • 1 heaped tsp jam or honey • 2 biscuits • half a slice of cake • 1 doughnut • 1 Danish pastry • 1 small bar of chocolate • 1 small tube or bag of sweets.

Too salty

Salt (sodium chloride) is essential for a variety of body functions, but we tend to eat too much through consumption of salty processed foods, 'fast' foods and ready-prepared foods, and by adding salt in cooking and at the table. The end result can be rising blood pressure as we get older, which puts us at higher risk of heart disease and stroke. Eating more vegetables and fruit increases potassium intake, which can help to counteract the damaging effects of salt.

Alcohol in a healthy diet

In recent research, moderate drinking of alcohol has been linked with a reduced risk of heart disease and stroke among men and women over 45. However, because of other risks associated with alcohol, particularly in excessive quantities, no doctor would recommend taking up drinking if you are teetotal. The healthiest pattern of drinking is to enjoy small amounts of alcohol with food, to have alcohol-free days and always to avoid getting drunk. A well-balanced diet is vital because nutrients from food (vitamins and minerals) are needed to detoxify the alcohol.

Water – the best choice

Drinking plenty of non-alcoholic liquid each day is an often overlooked part of a well-balanced diet. A minimum of 8 glasses (which is about 2 litres/3½ pints) is the ideal. If possible, these should not all be tea or coffee, as these are stimulants and diuretics, which cause the body to lose liquids, taking with them water-soluble vitamins. Water is the best choice. Other good choices are fruit or herb teas or tisanes, fruit juices – diluted with water, if preferred – or semi-skimmed milk (full-fat milk for very young children). Fizzy sugary or acidic drinks such as cola are more likely to damage tooth enamel than other drinks.

As a guide to the vitamin and mineral content of foods and recipes in the book, we have used the following terms and symbols, based on the percentage of the daily RNI provided by one serving for the average adult man or woman aged 19–49 years (see also pages 156–158):

✓✓✓ *or* excellent   at least 50% (half)

✓✓   *or* good   25–50% (one-quarter to one-half)

✓   *or* useful   10–25% (one-tenth to one-quarter)

Note that recipes contribute other nutrients, but the analyses only include those that provide at least 10% RNI per portion. Vitamins and minerals where deficiencies are rare are not included.

V denotes that a recipe is suitable for vegetarians.

Great Soups and Casseroles

Making the best of good ingredients

Soups and casseroles combine essential protein with protective vitamins, minerals and fibre in one healthy dish, retaining the nutrients in their delicious cooking liquid. They are wonderfully varied and can be served for all sorts of meals. Vegetables play a vital role, either as main ingredients or by bringing flavour, texture and colour to light seafood, tender poultry or long-simmered meats. Fresh or dried fruit, delicate herbs or powerful spices, seeds and nuts contribute their characteristics and particular benefits too. And with dumplings, pulses or grains, these dishes can become fabulous one-pot meals.

Healthy soups and casseroles

Soups and casseroles are ideal for well-balanced, easy eating. Full of good ingredients, they fit the bill for everyday meals and for special menus throughout the year. These dishes can satisfy robust appetites or appeal to delicate eaters, and they are popular with young and old alike. They can also be very low in fat and calories.

Rich in nutrients

An almost infinite variety of ingredients can be combined to make delicious and nutritious soups and casseroles. Most recipes contain several different vegetables, which offer a selection of vitamins, minerals and phytochemicals plus essential fibre. Fruit can be a surprise ingredient, contributing flavour and texture as well as its own vitamins, minerals and phytochemicals. Starchy foods, such as pasta, rice, grains and potatoes, are satisfying sources of energy, and meat, fish, poultry and pulses offer essential protein. Together, these ingredients can provide a well-balanced mixture of the vital nutrients needed for good health in a single, delicious serving.

Retaining the goodness

When food is cooked in liquid, the water-soluble vitamins – C and B complex – and some minerals seep from the food into the liquid. With soups and casseroles, all of the cooking liquid is retained as an integral part of the dish, so the nutrients are kept too.

Some nutrients are made more readily available to the body after long simmering, which is typical of many soups and casseroles. For example, the body can absorb the antioxidant beta-carotene more easily from cooked carrots than from raw ones, and the lycopene in tomatoes, believed to be a valuable anti-cancer agent, is enhanced by cooking.

◄◄ Clear soups, such as Oriental meatball broth (see page 76), can be packed with wholesome ingredients to make a hearty main dish

◄ Puréed soups are full of wonderful flavour. Smooth Tomato and pepper warmer (see page 28) is a perfect vitamin-rich winter's lunch

◄ Chilled soups, cooked or raw, are refreshing and light. Chilled leek and avocado soup (see page 94) is quick and easy to make, ideal for summer menus

Fuss-free cooking

Because soups and casseroles need minimum attention, they are practical for family meals and ideal for relaxed entertaining. In the simplest recipes everything goes into the pot to simmer from a 'cold start'. Others can be left to cook unattended after the ingredients have been briefly sweated or browned. Timing is rarely critical, so if you are not ready when the casserole is, it can be left to cook gently without spoiling. Also, soups and casseroles can often be made ahead and refrigerated, to be reheated at the last minute. Extra vitamin-rich vegetables added just before serving, or served as accompaniments, will provide fresh flavour and boost nutrients.

Soups for all seasons

Soups can be thick or thin, smooth or chunky, hot or cold. They are usually based on stock (made or bought) or water, but other liquids, such as milk, wine or fruit or vegetable juices, can be used to enrich or intensify the flavour. The texture can be changed by thickening with healthy starchy ingredients such as potatoes, bread or flour, or by puréeing.

Soups come in many appealing forms. Broths are clear and unthickened, and may contain chunky ingredients. Puréed soups can be coarse or ultra smooth. Chowder, traditionally made from fish or seafood, is a satisfyingly chunky soup.

Moist, gentle cooking

Unlike sauced dishes, where liquid is added towards the end of the cooking, for stews and casseroles the ingredients are cooked in the liquid for most or all of the cooking time, simmered in a tightly covered pot in the oven or on the hob. Just about anything can be cooked in this convenient way, from joints of meat and whole birds or fish to lean steaks, chunks of vegetables, grains, pulses and dried fruit.

Stewing implies long, slow cooking, to tenderise tough cuts of meat and allow the flavours of the ingredients to blend. Braising is the same, but uses less liquid. Casseroles are very similar to stews – indeed the two terms are used almost interchangeably – the main difference being that casseroles are usually not cooked for such a long time. A ragout is an especially rich casserole. In hotpots, potatoes often play a starring role – layered with ingredients or added towards the end of cooking, they help to create one-pot main courses.

◄ Bring additional vegetable goodness to traditional meat stews – try Beef in red wine (see page 136), full of tender baby vegetables

◄ Combine delicate fish and seasonal vegetables, as in Summer salmon and asparagus (see page 96), for a quick-cook casserole

▼ Take a variety of vegetables for everyday meals – Braised vegetables with falafel and yogurt sauce (see page 154) makes a vegetarian feast

Pots of goodness

The exciting thing about soups and casseroles is that they are endlessly versatile. Imaginative combinations of vegetables cooked with fish, poultry, meat or pulses create appetising dishes packed with vitamins and minerals as well as protein. With starchy foods included or alongside, they make delicious, satisfying meals.

Make the most of vegetables

In addition to their vital vitamins, minerals, phytochemicals and fibre, vegetables bring flavour, texture and visual appeal to soups and casseroles. Onions, carrots and celery are the basic flavourings, and to these you can add a wonderful variety of other vegetables. As an added bonus, this will help you to meet the 5-a-day fruit and vegetable challenge.

- Stir in roots, such as turnips and swede, early in cooking.
- Peppers, celery and fennel are superb when long braised.
- Cauliflower, broccoli, green beans, peas, spinach and other leafy greens bring freshness in the final stages.
- A mixture of root and leafy vegetables balances the richness of meat and game.
- Lighter, crisp vegetables complement delicate fish – try peppers, fennel, Swiss chard, mustard greens or pak choy.

Orange and dark green vegetables, such as carrots, swede and broccoli, provide the antioxidant beta-carotene, which helps to protect against certain types of cancer, while leafy vegetables offer B-complex vitamins, which are involved in releasing energy from food. All vegetables contain vital vitamin C as well as many disease-preventing phytochemicals and both soluble and insoluble fibre.

Better fresh than frozen?

Vegetables are frozen in peak condition and their vitamin content does not diminish significantly during freezing. They often provide more goodness than 'fresh' produce that is slightly stale. Frozen peas, beans, Brussels sprouts, broccoli, sweetcorn and spinach are great ingredients for soups and casseroles, as are frozen mixed vegetables.

Don't forget fruit

Fruit is a great ingredient for bringing sweet, fresh flavour to savoury casseroles and it makes super-refreshing soups. The

Vegetables

Fruit

vitamin, mineral and phytochemical value of fruit is as powerful as that of vegetables.

- Apples, pears, plums, apricots and pineapple complement rich meat or poultry. Add them to casseroles early in cooking or towards the end as a refreshing garnish.
- Citrus flavours are international favourites and scented exotic fruits are refreshing partners for herbs and spices.
- Cranberries and redcurrants are as good frozen as fresh and they are popular in savoury dishes. Try other berries too – raspberries are good with game, blackcurrants with rich venison or lamb.
- Dried fruit can enrich casseroles – especially when paired with red wine or cider to give a deliciously intense flavour.

Protein: a little does you good

In a healthy well-balanced diet, protein-rich foods, such as meat, poultry and fish, are eaten sparingly, complemented by plenty of vegetables and starchy foods.

Poultry, game and meat bring inimitable flavour to many casseroles and soups, either as ingredients or as the basis of stock. They also bring vital protein and other nutrients, such as B vitamins, zinc and iron. Tougher cuts are economical and excellent when long cooked. Expensive, lean cuts are quick and easy to prepare and cook – they can be extended with starchy grains, rice and pasta.

Fish and seafood are excellent low-fat protein foods for soups and casseroles. They provide vitamin B_{12}, for a healthy nervous system, and the mineral iodine. Oily fish, such as mackerel and salmon, are a source of omega-3 fatty acids, which make a positive contribution to cardiovascular health.

Pulses (beans and lentils) provide protein as well as fibre, B vitamins, and iron and other minerals. Dried pulses are ideal in soups and casseroles, although canned versions are convenient when time is short and are just as nutritious.

Firm tofu, a low-fat protein food made from soya beans, retains its shape well in clear soups and vegetable casseroles. It is a useful source of calcium, which is essential for strong bones and teeth, and of phytoestrogens, which are thought to help protect against some forms of cancer. Tofu may also have a role to play in preventing heart disease.

Satisfying starch

The starchy (complex carbohydrate) foods such as potatoes, pasta, rice and other grains are excellent cooked in delicious broth or the liquor in a casserole. Add them to make a substantial first-course soup or one-pot main course.

- Long-grain white or brown rice and wild rice give a nutty taste and texture to clear and puréed soups.
- Pasta can be added to soups for the last 10–15 minutes of cooking. Use tiny shapes (*pastina*) such as orzo or ditalini.
- Cover casseroles with a thick layer of sliced potatoes or sweet potatoes, or cook scones on the top to make a cobbler.
- Ring the changes by using pearl barley, which is ideal for long, gentle cooking.

Protein-rich foods

Satisfying starches and nutritious pulses

Simply nutritious

Preparation and cooking methods that retain the maximum nutrients, for the best possible food value in a dish, are often the same ones that enhance the flavours of ingredients. Making delicious and healthy soups and casseroles is not difficult, because these techniques are also often the quickest and easiest.

Golden rules for preparation

- Rinse vegetables and fresh fruit thoroughly just before cooking. Don't leave them to soak because water-soluble vitamins will seep out and then be discarded with the water.
- Useful quantities of nutrients are found just under the skin of many vegetables and fruit, and the skin provides valuable fibre. So when possible, wash or scrub vegetables and fruit, rather than peeling them.
- When peeling is essential, remove the thinnest possible layer. Remember, too, that vegetable trimmings (including onion skins) make good stock.
- Trim all visible fat from meat and poultry, and remove the skin from poultry, to keep fat to a minimum.

Simple cutting

Soups and casseroles are so nutritious because they retain the soluble nutrients – the B vitamins, vitamin C and some minerals – that are often discarded with the cooking water.

Cutting ingredients into large, rather than fine, pieces means there is less surface area from which nutrients can be lost. This also helps to preserve the heat-sensitive B vitamins and vitamin C, which can be destroyed by very high temperatures or during prolonged cooking.

When adding everything at once, cut tough foods into smaller pieces than items that cook quickly. Cutting meat across the grain will make it more tender when cooked.

Softening and sweating

Most savoury dishes start with onions being cooked briefly to take the raw 'edge' off their flavour and soften them. Garlic and other vegetables, such as celery and carrot, are often added. Softening needs only the minimum of oil, plus frequent stirring to prevent the onions from burning. Another method is to 'sweat' the onions in their own juice. Cook for a few seconds in a tiny amount of oil, then cover the pan and reduce the heat to very low. Continue cooking until the onions are soft and translucent, which can take 10 minutes.

Cut ingredients of similar texture into equal pieces to ensure even cooking

Browning and deglazing for richer flavour

Browning meat and vegetables before adding liquid enhances the colour of a soup or stew and adds a rich flavour. With meat, the browning, or 'searing', is for improving colour and flavour, not for sealing in the juices. Use the minimum of oil and a high heat to brown meat quickly, stirring and turning it so that all surfaces are coloured. As long as the meat is not burnt or charred, this is a good way to achieve maximum flavour from a small amount of meat.

If your stew pot or casserole is not flameproof, and you are browning the ingredients in a frying pan, be sure to deglaze the pan and then add the liquid to the stew pot. To deglaze, add a little wine, stock or water and bring to the boil, scraping up the browned bits from the bottom of the pan.

Starting cold

When you want to emphasise the natural flavours and colours of the ingredients in a soup or casserole, rather than the flavours and colours that result from browning, you can use the 'cold start' method. For this, the initial softening or sweating of onions and other aromatics may be very brief or omitted altogether. Instead, all the ingredients are just put into the pot at the same time and brought to a simmer together. As they simmer, they gradually become tender and the flavours mingle deliciously.

Gentle simmering and skimming

After bringing a soup or stew to the boil, reduce the heat and simmer gently for optimum flavour and texture – if cooked at a full boil, the ingredients roll around and may start to disintegrate before they are cooked through. Gentle cooking also helps to preserve heat-sensitive nutrients.

Soups and casseroles made with fish and seafood tend to be cooked briefly. When used in longer-cooked dishes, fish and other delicate ingredients, such as tender vegetables, are best added in stages or towards the end of cooking.

Remove scum that surfaces as broth heats and skim off any fat at the end of cooking. Kitchen paper is useful for mopping up small amounts of fat, especially on chunky casseroles. Fat from poultry and meat congeals when chilled, and can then be lifted off easily from the surface and discarded, which is useful for stocks, soups and stews that can be reheated for serving.

▲ Soften onions in their own juices or with the minimum of oil
▼ Brown meat quickly before cooking for rich flavour and colour

▼ Pre-cooking is not always necessary – add raw ingredients or frozen vegetables straight to the cooking liquid for fresh flavour

Fabulous flavours

The ingredients for soups and casseroles offer a wonderful range of intrinsic flavours. Seasoned marinades and dry 'rubs' can enhance them, or they can be complemented by adding aromatic herbs and spices, rich nut or fruit pastes, mustards and vinegars. Just a little can add zest and be a healthy alternative to lots of salt.

Versatile herbs

The bright colours, varied flavours and delicious scent of herbs can elevate the taste of the simplest soup or casserole. Whether used singly or in combination, fresh, frozen or dried, herbs are a pleasing addition to a dish. Although normally used in small quantities, fresh herbs can contribute to the nutritional quality of your diet if eaten regularly or used very generously.

For a deep, pervasive flavour, add herbs early in cooking. Mix them in at the end for fresh or pungent overtones. Add sprigs for a subtle flavour, chopped herbs for a more intense infusion – cutting them releases more of their essential oils. Use dried herbs in long-simmered dishes. Delicate fresh herbs such as basil and chervil, which lose much of their flavour when heated, are best sprinkled over just before serving.

Aromatic spices

Like herbs, the distinctive colours, flavours and scents of spices enhance other foods and also stimulate the appetite. Most spices are used dried, exceptions being root ginger and chillies. When whole, dried spices – such as cinnamon sticks, whole cloves, star anise, coriander seeds and juniper berries, for example – make a subtle flavour contribution compared to their ground equivalents. Small seeds, such as cumin, caraway and mustard, also offer appealing texture.

The flavour of dried spices can be made rounder and richer by 'roasting' them. Cook whole spices or spice seeds in a dry heavy-based pan over a gentle heat, shaking or stirring them

Adding dried spices or fresh root ginger to a simple stew or casserole will boost the flavour

frequently, until very lightly coloured and aromatic. Small seeds, such as cumin, will begin to 'pop' when ready. The spices can be left whole, or ground in an electric mill or with a pestle and mortar. Roasted ground spices do not taste raw, so they can be sprinkled over food towards the end of cooking.

Whole spices are often removed at the end of the cooking time. To make this easy, tie the spices in a piece of muslin.

Punchy pastes

Herbs, spices, nuts and seeds can be ground and blended with a little plain low-fat yogurt, vinegar (balsamic vinegar is especially good), extra virgin olive oil or fruit juice to make delicious flavouring pastes. Swirl a spoonful or two into a finished soup or casserole to add extra flavour and colour and an enticing aroma. Nut and seed pastes will add protein too, as well as vitamins and fibre.

Yogurt and lemon juice are the classic base for Indian spice pastes; yogurt is also good mixed with herbs, citrus zest and ground nuts. A yogurt-based paste will add less fat than a swirl of cream and also contributes some calcium.

Classic nut pastes use lots of oil, but apple juice also works well for a lower fat result, particularly with walnuts, cashews, sunflower seeds or sesame seeds. Simply grind the nuts or seeds in a blender, then trickle in the juice with the motor running. As a guide, allow about 100 ml (3½ fl oz) juice to 50 g (1¾ oz) nuts.

Sweet-sour fruit pastes add intense flavour. Dried apricots are terrific puréed with orange or lemon zest and juice, herbs or spices. A little wine, sherry, cider vinegar or balsamic vinegar can be added too, especially with sweet fruit, such as prunes or dried pears.

Marinades and dry rubs

Steeping food in a seasoning mixture before cooking is a very good way to add flavour. Marinades, which are seasoned liquids, can also add moisture and help to tenderise tough ingredients such as older game birds and cheap cuts of meat. To retain any nutrients that might have leached into the marinade, be sure to use the liquid in the dish.

Marinades usually contain acid ingredients such as wine, vinegar or lemon juice, as these have tenderising properties. They may also be based on yogurt or fresh papaya or pineapple, all of which contain an enzyme that tenderises meat. Marinades also normally contain a little oil and aromatics such as onion, garlic, citrus zest, herbs and spices. After marinating, food that is to be browned should be drained and dried thoroughly.

Dry marinades or 'rubs' are mixtures of dry ingredients, such as herbs and spices. Citrus zest or spring onions can also be added. Rubs are spread directly on the food.

Making a bouquet garni

This is a classic herb flavouring, traditionally consisting of 2 sprigs of parsley, 1 sprig of thyme and a bay leaf, tied together with string. Parsley stalks are often used and many other combinations of herbs can be prepared. For example, celery is often included for flavouring chicken or turkey, fennel for fish, rosemary instead of thyme for game, oregano or marjoram for root vegetables, and sage for pork. Orange or lemon zest can also be added for beef, game or pork. Whole spices, such as juniper berries or cloves, can be included when the herbs are tied in a piece of muslin. The possibilities are almost endless. Dried bouquet garni sachets are also available.

Flavour carriers

Oils and vinegars flavoured with aromatics, such as herbs, spices and citrus zests, or with berry fruits, can add a last-minute zing to a soup or casserole. Just a little drizzle or swirl is all that is needed.

Flavoured oils and vinegars are easy and economical to make, using roasted whole spices, fresh chillies, fresh or dried herbs, raspberries and so on. Vinegars keep for months in a cool dark place. Oils flavoured with fresh herbs will keep in the refrigerator for up to 2 weeks.

Finishing touches

Nowadays, lighter cooking liquors tend to have more appeal than rich, heavy sauces. The traditional creamy finish is being supplanted by healthier ways to thicken soups and casseroles – all just as delicious. And there are many lower fat methods of enriching or intensifying the flavour at the last minute.

Thickening tricks

Many traditional recipes for soups and casseroles start with a flour base – a roux of butter and flour, meat tossed in flour, flour stirred into softened onions. When cooking stewing cuts of meat during subsequent cooking, as well as thickening the liquid, the flour absorbs some excess fat in the dish. For a lower fat result, it is often better to thicken soups and casseroles at the end of cooking, once any excess fat has been skimmed off.

- **Beurre manié** is a classic thickener made by mixing equal quantities of butter and flour into a thick paste. This is whisked into simmering liquid in small lumps, allowing each to be absorbed before adding the next. Simmer, stirring occasionally, for 3 minutes. As a guide, 30 g (1 oz) each of butter and plain flour will lightly thicken 600 ml (1 pint) of liquid. Beurre manié is useful for thin soups and casseroles where little fat has been used at the beginning of cooking.
- **Flour and cornflour** are fat-free thickeners, ideal for meat casseroles. Sprinkle plain flour into a little cold liquid, whisk until smooth and then whisk into the hot soup or sauce. Allow about 30 g (1 oz) plain flour to lightly thicken 600 ml (1 pint) liquid. Mix cornflour to a paste with a little cold liquid, then add a ladleful of the hot liquid. Stir this mixture into the cooking liquid. Bring to the boil, stirring, and simmer for 3 minutes. As a guide, 3 tbsp cornflour will thicken 600 ml (1 pint) liquid.
- **Potatoes and other root vegetables** are nutritious in soups and casseroles, and they can thicken them too. Purée the entire pot of soup, or just a portion if you don't want such a smooth result. You can also mash ingredients in the pot with a potato masher or fork. Butter beans, lentils, chickpeas and other pulses – good sources of protein and fibre – can also be mashed or puréed with the cooking liquid.
- **Breadcrumbs** offer starchy carbohydrate as well as thickening power. Whisk them into the liquid and simmer, still whisking, for about 5 minutes. Allow about 50 g (1¾ oz) fresh breadcrumbs to 600 ml (1 pint) liquid.
- **Cereals** are natural and nutritious thickeners. Oatmeal, a good source of soluble fibre, gives a rustic finish to hearty soups and casseroles. Whisk medium or fine oatmeal into barely simmering liquid, then bring to the boil, still whisking, and simmer for 10 minutes. Allow 2 tbsp oatmeal to lightly thicken 600 ml (1 pint) liquid. Corn meal (maize meal) and couscous can also be used – 30 g (1 oz) is needed for each 600 ml (1 pint) of liquid, and 15 minutes simmering.
- **Egg yolks and cream**, mixed together in a liaison, make a classic thickener. Although high in fat, it is used in small quantities, and the egg yolks contribute vitamins, minerals and protein. Allow 2 egg yolks and 4 tbsp crème fraîche or single cream to 600 ml (1 pint) liquid. Whisk the yolks lightly with the cream and about 6 tbsp of the hot liquid, then add to the soup or sauce and heat gently without boiling. Egg yolks can be used on their own, in the same way.

Enriching or intensifying the flavour

Enriching a soup or casserole at the last minute can add greatly to its appeal. This can be as simple as a small knob of butter, a little cream or a swirl of a flavoured oil. The enrichment need not be high in fat as only a small amount is needed, and there are lots of alternatives to rich cream. For example, yogurt and fromage frais contain considerably less fat than double cream. These should be added off the heat, just before serving, as they curdle easily if heated.

To intensify flavour you can simply boil the cooking liquid after the solid ingredients are removed, to reduce it in volume. A splash of wine or brandy can also be added.

◄◄ A liaison of egg yolks and cream will thicken and enrich a soup or sauce

◄ For smooth results, blend cornflour with a little cold liquid before ladling in some of the hot liquid

▼ Try cereals and grains for hearty, well-thickened soups or casseroles

► Purée or mash pulses with their cooking liquid to thicken soups and stews

►► Stir in fresh breadcrumbs, then simmer until smooth and creamy

► For beurre manié, mix equal quantities of flour and butter to a paste

►► Boil cooking liquid to reduce and concentrate its flavour, adding a little wine for extra taste

Perfect partners

The ingredients in a soup or casserole and the accompaniments served alongside need to be carefully chosen for complementary and contrasting flavours, colours and textures, as well as for the nutritional balance of the meal. Aim for variety, including both raw and cooked foods to enjoy interesting, healthy eating.

The easy choice: bread

Bread is an unbeatable and easy partner for a soup or casserole and adds low-fat starchy carbohydrate to the meal. Bread is also a good source of important nutrients, including B vitamins and calcium. French, wholemeal, rye, mixed-grain and soda breads can all be enjoyed in generous portions.

Flat breads – pitta, naan, chapattis and flour tortillas – are ideal for dipping in soups and scooping up casseroles. Try warm muffins, crumpets, scones, potato scones and plain (unsweetened) drop scones or thick pancakes too.

Sustaining potatoes

Potatoes are another excellent source of satisfying starch. Boiled or baked in their jackets, lightly crushed or mashed, they are a firm favourite with casseroles. They can be served with soups too – just place a mound of creamy, herb-seasoned mash in the bowl before ladling in a smooth, full-flavoured soup. Or serve crisp-baked potato wedges alongside.

Chopped fresh herbs, softened garlic and mustard are all popular additions to mashed potatoes, but you can also stir in vitamin-rich raw or lightly cooked vegetables for added colour and texture (this is a good way to get children to eat more vegetables). Use just one vegetable or a mixture – chopped blanched broccoli, diced tomatoes, shredded raw spinach, grated raw beetroot or carrots, finely shredded fennel or celery are all good. Chopped watercress, rocket, parsley, spring onions and grated dessert apple are also delicious.

Substantial starches

Sample the many types of rice, including wild and brown rice for important fibre and B vitamins. Wheat, pearl or pot barley and buckwheat can be served individually or combined with rice. Couscous is ideal for absorbing thin sauces.

When cooking rice and other grains, add lemongrass, bay leaves, a cinnamon stick, a few green cardamom pods or toasted fennel seeds to the cooking water. Toss toasted cumin seeds or chopped nuts into the cooked grains or couscous.

Pasta, in all its myriad shapes, is another popular starchy food to serve with casseroles. As with breads and grains, wholegrain varieties offer more vitamins and fibre.

Accompaniments can turn a soup or a casserole into a complete meal

Pleasing contrasts

Fresh fruit and vegetables bring extra vitamins and vitality to long-cooked dishes. Serve them in finely cut salads or make them into salsas, fresh chutneys and raitas to add a new dimension in temperature and texture contrast. Use powerful ingredients, herbs and spices, and make generous amounts so that everyone has plenty.

- For a nutrient-packed salsa, mix diced ingredients such as tomatoes, fresh chillies, peppers, celery, onion, garlic, dessert apple and mango. Red peppers, tomatoes and mangoes all provide beta-carotene and vitamin C. Onions and garlic have many beneficial properties.
- For a flavour-balanced relish, combine sweet fruit with savoury ingredients and sharp citrus juice, vinegar or yogurt.
- Make a tangy relish with tart cranberries or sharp redcurrants, both packed with vitamin C.
- For an Oriental-style salad, finely shred radishes, cucumber, courgette, spring onions and mustard greens, and mix with a few drops of sesame oil and a sprinkling of soy sauce.
- For a raita, add plenty of grated vegetables and fruit to plain low-fat yogurt. Papaya, peaches or mango are good with cucumber, carrot, peppers, spinach and watercress.

Vegetable variety

Experiment with the range of vegetables now available to create colourful accompaniments for casseroles. Try sizzling side dishes such as freshly stir-fried vegetables, or braise vegetables in the oven alongside the stew pot. Serve boiled, steamed, grilled or roasted vegetables, varying the cooking methods for interesting meals. When boiling or steaming crisp green and yellow vegetables, be sure not to overcook as this destroys vitamins.

Nutritious garnishes

There are many garnishes that can add to the visual appeal as well as contributing goodness.

- A sprinkling of crunchy pine nuts, sesame seeds, sunflower seeds, chopped walnuts, and flaked or slivered almonds adds a contrast in texture to smooth soups. They are all useful sources of protein and also provide vitamin E, some of the B-group vitamins and a variety of minerals. They are high in fat, but this is mostly the healthy, unsaturated type. For the best flavour and crunch, lightly toast nuts and seeds in a dry frying pan, stirring frequently.
- Make crisp croutons to sprinkle over a soup or casserole, and add some starchy carbohydrate too. Brush slices of bread very lightly on both sides with extra virgin olive oil – allow 1 tbsp oil to 2 slices of bread to garnish 4 portions. Cut thick slices or use French bread or ciabatta to make chunky croutons for rustic soups and stews. Lightly brown the bread on both sides in a dry frying pan, then remove and cut into cubes. Return to the pan and cook gently, turning often, until crisp. Croutons can be tossed with chopped fresh herbs or grated citrus zest for extra flavour.
- Vitamin-rich vegetables – in fine strips or coarsely grated – will add fresh colour, texture and flavour to soups and casseroles. Carrots, cucumber, peppers, celery, fennel, spring onions and radishes are all excellent raw vegetable garnishes. Sprigs of watercress, shredded spinach or chicory and tiny florets of broccoli work well, too. Take extra portions of vegetable garnishes to the table so that more can be added.
- Fresh fruit garnishes, packed with vitamins, can complement all kinds of soups and casseroles. For fish and seafood, use orange or grapefruit segments as well as the familiar lemon wedges (for their juice). Neat pieces of peach, plum, apricot, apple, pear and banana – tossed in lemon juice to prevent discoloration – can garnish meat, poultry and vegetable dishes. Pomegranate seeds, pineapple, mango and lychees taste terrific with most savoury foods, and berries – raspberries, blueberries and blackcurrants or redcurrants – are excellent with poultry and game.

Basic stock recipes

Stock is simple to make and freezes well; it also retains valuable water-soluble vitamins. Here are basic recipes that can be varied according to the ingredients available – a poultry carcass, bones from a joint of meat, even fresh vegetable trimmings. Add your favourite herbs or spices to boost the flavour.

Good ingredients

Vegetables are essential in all stocks. Onions, carrots and celery are the basics, but leeks, root vegetables and the stalks from cabbage, cauliflower or broccoli all contribute flavour – and vitamins. Strong-tasting vegetables, such as parsnips, swedes or Brussels sprouts, can dominate, so add them only when their flavour is required. There is no need to peel vegetables for stock, and vegetable peelings can be added too – onion skins add wonderful colour.

Meat bones and poultry carcasses can be used raw or cooked, but they should always be fresh. They make stock richer in B vitamins. Poultry portions can be used when a carcass is not available, and inexpensive cuts of meat such as stewing beef or lamb are alternatives to bones. Trim off all the visible fat from meat before cooking and be sure to skim the stock well.

Bay leaves and parsley are the essential flavouring herbs. Thyme is also often added and other herbs can be used according to the flavour required. A strip of pared lemon zest and a garlic clove are also excellent.

Using home-made stock is the best way to ensure the most delicious results

A great freezer standby

Pour the cooled, well-skimmed stock into rigid freezerproof containers, filling them only three-quarters full because the stock expands on freezing. Chill, then skim off any remaining fat. Cover with airtight lids and freeze. Vegetable, poultry and beef stock can be frozen for up to 6 months. Ham stock should be used within 1 month. When required, simply heat the frozen stock until melted, then bring to the boil.

Alternatives to making stock

Many excellent soups and casseroles can be made without stock – vegetables, herbs and other aromatics all contribute plenty of flavour, so water is often the only liquid needed. In other recipes, fruit juices, wine, cider, beer and other liquids contribute their own delicious flavours.

When a recipe calls for stock and you don't have any in the refrigerator or freezer, you can use bought chilled fresh stocks, bouillon powders or pastes and good-quality stock cubes. These are particularly useful for quick, everyday dishes.

Light vegetable stock

This light stock is suitable for vegetarian dishes and for fish, poultry or meat recipes when a delicate flavour is required.

Makes about 1.7 litres (3 pints)
1 tbsp sunflower oil
225 g (8 oz) leeks, chopped
1 large onion, chopped
1 large bay leaf
several sprigs of fresh thyme
several sprigs of parsley, stalks bruised
225 g (8 oz) carrots, diced
3 large celery sticks with any leaves, diced
1 tsp salt
5 black peppercorns

Preparation time: 15 minutes
Cooking time: about 1 hour

1 Heat the oil in a large heavy-based saucepan or stockpot. Add the leeks and onion, stir well and reduce the heat to low. Cover with a tight-fitting lid and leave the vegetables to sweat for about 20 minutes, shaking the pan occasionally but without lifting the lid.
2 Add the bay leaf, thyme, parsley, carrots, celery and salt. Pour in 2 litres (3½ pints) cold water and increase the heat to high. Bring slowly to the boil, skimming the surface of the liquid to remove any scum.
3 As soon as the water boils and all the scum has been removed, add the peppercorns and reduce the heat to low. Cover and simmer for 35 minutes.
4 Strain the stock into a large, heatproof bowl and set it aside to cool. Use at once or cool and then chill until required.

Rich vegetable stock

This stock is excellent in meat soups and casseroles, and is ideal for hearty vegetarian recipes.

Makes about 1.7 litres (3 pints)
125 g (4½ oz) whole wheat grains
1 tbsp sunflower oil
125 g (4½ oz) dark flat mushrooms, chopped
2 onions, chopped
3 carrots, chopped
3 celery sticks, chopped
1 sprig of parsley, stalk bruised
1 sprig of fresh thyme
1 sprig of fresh marjoram
2 bay leaves
8 black peppercorns
1 tsp salt

Preparation time: 55 minutes
Cooking time: 55 minutes

1 Preheat the oven to 180°C (350°F, gas mark 4). Put the wheat in a roasting tin and roast for 30 minutes or until the grains are dark brown.
2 Heat the oil in a large heavy-based saucepan over a low heat. Add the mushrooms and onions and stir to coat them in the oil. Cover the pan and sweat the vegetables for 5 minutes, shaking the pan occasionally.
3 Stir in the roasted wheat, carrots and celery. Pour in 2 litres (3½ pints) water, increase the heat to high and bring to the boil, skimming off any scum that rises to the surface.
4 Reduce the heat. Add the parsley, thyme, marjoram, bay leaves, peppercorns and salt. Cover the pan and simmer for 45 minutes.
5 Strain the stock through a fine sieve into a heatproof bowl. Use at once or leave to cool, then chill until required.

Fish stock

Makes about 1.2 litres (2 pints)

1 onion, thinly sliced
4 sprigs of parsley
2 bay leaves
2 carrots, thinly sliced
2 celery sticks, thinly sliced
4 black peppercorns
900 g (2 lb) trimmings from white fish, including skin, bones, and
  heads without gills
1.3 litres (2¼ pints) boiling water

Preparation time: 10 minutes, plus 10 minutes cooling
Cooking time: 35 minutes

1 Place the onion, parsley, bay leaves, carrots, celery, peppercorns and fish trimmings in a large saucepan. Pour in the boiling water. Bring back to the boil, then reduce the heat and simmer gently for 30 minutes.
2 Remove from the heat and leave to cool for 10 minutes, then strain the stock through a fine sieve into a heatproof bowl. Discard the fish trimmings and vegetables. Use at once or cool and chill.

Another idea

• Use 400 g (14 oz) inexpensive white fish fillet, such as pollock, instead of the trimmings.

Chicken stock

Makes about 1.4 litres (2½ pints)

1 chicken carcass or the bones from 4 chicken pieces, cooked or raw,
  or 1 raw chicken leg quarter, about 250 g (8½ oz)
1 onion, quartered
1 large carrot, roughly chopped
1 celery stick, cut into chunks
1 bay leaf
1 sprig of parsley, stalk bruised
1 sprig of fresh thyme
8 black peppercorns
½ tsp salt

Preparation time: 10 minutes, plus cooling
Cooking time: about 2 hours

1 Break up the chicken carcass or bones; leave the leg joint whole. Place in a large saucepan. Add the onion, carrot and celery. Pour in 2 litres (3½ pints) water and bring to the boil over a high heat, skimming off any scum from the surface.
2 Add the bay leaf, parsley, thyme, peppercorns and salt. Reduce the heat, cover and simmer gently for 2 hours.
3 Strain the stock through a sieve into a heatproof bowl, discarding the bones or joint and vegetables. Cool and chill the stock, then skim off any fat that sets on the surface.

Some more ideas

• To make turkey stock, use a turkey carcass. For game stock, use the carcass from 1–2 cooked game birds.

Beef stock

Makes about 1.4 litres (2½ pints)

1 tbsp sunflower oil
125 g (4½ oz) lean stewing beef in one piece
1 onion, quartered
1 carrot, roughly chopped
1 celery stick, roughly chopped
2 bay leaves
1 sprig of parsley, stalk bruised
1 sprig of fresh thyme
10 black peppercorns
½ tsp salt

Preparation time: 10 minutes, plus cooling
Cooking time: 2¼ hours

1 Heat the oil in a large saucepan over a high heat. Brown the beef on both sides, then remove it and set aside.
2 Reduce the heat and add the vegetables. Cook gently, stirring occasionally, until browned. Pour in 2 litres (3½ pints) water and bring to the boil.
3 Replace the beef and heat until the liquid is simmering. Skim off any scum, then add the herbs, peppercorns and salt. Reduce the heat, cover and leave to bubble for 2 hours.
4 Strain the stock through a sieve into a heatproof bowl. Discard the beef and vegetables. Cool and chill the stock, then skim off any fat from the surface.

Some more ideas
• For lamb or pork stock, use lean lamb or pork. Leftovers from a joint on the bone can be used instead of fresh meat.

Ham stock

Makes about 2 litres (3½ pints)

1 meaty knuckle bone from a cooked ham
1 onion, quartered
1 carrot, roughly chopped
1 celery stick, roughly chopped
1 bay leaf
1 sprig of parsley, stalk bruised
2 fresh sage leaves
4 cloves
8 black peppercorns

Preparation time: 10 minutes, plus cooling
Cooking time: about 2 hours

1 Place the ham bone, onion, carrot and celery in a large saucepan. Pour in 2.5 litres (4½ pints) cold water. Bring to the boil over a high heat, skimming off any scum.
2 Add the bay leaf, parsley, sage, cloves and peppercorns, then reduce the heat so that the liquid simmers gently. Cover the pan and leave the stock to bubble for 2 hours.
3 Strain the stock through a sieve into a heatproof bowl. Discard the bone and the vegetables. Cool and chill, then skim off any fat from the surface of the stock.

Some more ideas
• Beef or lamb bones from a roast joint can be used instead of the ham bone.

Light Soups

Full of zest and flavour

Soup can make a fabulous first impression without being too filling. Try a seafood broth or full-flavoured prawn bisque for a starter, or savour the benefits of colourful vegetables in a smooth tomato and pepper soup. Warm up lunchtime with a delicious broth of turkey and vegetables, herb-scented ham and pea soup or a chunky chicken and potato chowder that will be popular with all the family. When the weather is hot, cool down with Spanish-style crunchy gazpacho, or fragrant melon soup with succulent summer berries.

And for the ultimate pick-me-up, enjoy a high-vitality soup with its luscious mix of exotic fruit and refreshing vegetables.

Tomato and pepper warmer

Sweet red peppers and passata make a beautiful red soup that is sophisticated yet simple to prepare. Swirled with crème fraîche and accompanied by hot pesto bread, it makes a splendid special-occasion starter. For a mid-week supper, garnish the soup with fresh herbs instead of crème fraîche and serve with wholemeal bread.

Serves 6

1 long French loaf

3 tbsp pesto

2 tbsp extra virgin olive oil

1 onion, coarsely chopped

1 garlic clove, chopped

675 g (1½ lb) red peppers (3–4 peppers, depending on size), seeded and coarsely chopped

300 ml (10 fl oz) vegetable stock, preferably home-made light or rich (see page 23)

300 ml (10 fl oz) passata

1 tsp chopped fresh thyme or ½ tsp dried thyme

¼ tsp ground cinnamon

1 tsp sugar

salt and pepper

To garnish

6 tbsp crème fraîche

6 sprigs of fresh basil

Preparation and cooking time: about 50 minutes

Each serving provides

kcal 340, **protein** 8 g, **fat** 14 g (of which saturated fat 2 g), **carbohydrate** 44 g (of which sugars 11 g), **fibre** 4 g

✓✓✓	A, C
✓✓	B₁, folate
✓	niacin

1 Preheat the oven to 180°C (350°F, gas mark 4). Cut the French loaf across in half so that it will fit into the oven. Cut each half into 3.5 cm (1½ in) thick slices, leaving the slices attached at the base. Hold the slices apart and spread each one thinly with pesto, then press them back together. Wrap the bread in foil and set aside.

2 Heat the oil in a saucepan. Add the onion and garlic and fry gently for 5 minutes or until softened but not browned. Stir in the peppers and cook for a further 5 minutes, stirring occasionally. Pour in the stock and remove from the heat.

3 Place the bread in the oven to heat for 15 minutes. Meanwhile, purée the soup in a blender until smooth. Return the soup to the pan and stir in the passata, thyme, cinnamon and sugar. Heat the soup gently without allowing it to boil. Season to taste.

4 Ladle the soup into warm bowls and garnish each portion with a spoonful of crème fraîche and a sprig of basil. Serve with the hot pesto bread.

Some more ideas

• Plain low-fat yogurt or fromage frais can be used instead of crème fraîche.

• For a spicy version, add 1 seeded and finely chopped fresh red chilli with the onion, or a dash of Tabasco or other chilli sauce with the final seasoning.

• For a tomato and carrot soup, use 675 g (1½ lb) diced carrots instead of the red peppers. After the stock is added, cover the pan and simmer the carrots for 10 minutes or until they are tender. Finish as in the main recipe, omitting the sugar.

• Add 450 g (1 lb) coarsely chopped leeks and 4 sliced celery sticks with the onion instead of the red peppers. Cook for about 15 minutes or until the leeks are softened before adding the stock. Purée the soup and finish as in the main recipe, omitting the sugar.

Plus points

• Red peppers are an excellent source of vitamin C – weight for weight they contain over twice as much vitamin C as oranges. They also provide good amounts of carotenoids and bioflavonoids – both antioxidants that help to protect against heart disease and cancer.

• Tomatoes contain lycopene, a carotenoid compound and a valuable antioxidant that is thought to help protect against prostate cancer. Lycopene is enhanced by cooking and so is most readily available in processed tomato products, such as canned tomatoes, tomato purée and passata.

Artichoke soup with caraway

Looking like knobbly new potatoes, Jerusalem artichokes have a distinctive, yet delicate, flavour that goes well with other root vegetables, particularly in a smooth-textured soup. Sweetly aromatic caraway seeds complement the vegetable flavours and transform an unassuming, familiar dish into something rather special.

Serves 6

1 tbsp lemon juice

500 g (1 lb 2 oz) Jerusalem artichokes

15 g (½ oz) butter

1 celery stick, chopped

1 small onion, chopped

2 carrots, chopped

1 garlic clove, chopped

1.2 litres (2 pints) chicken stock, preferably home-made (see page 24)

1 tsp caraway seeds

150 ml (5 fl oz) semi-skimmed milk

4 tbsp single cream

salt and pepper

To garnish

1 small carrot

2–3 tbsp chopped parsley

Preparation time: about 15 minutes

Cooking time: about 40 minutes

Each serving provides

kcal 103, **protein** 4 g, **fat** 5 g (of which saturated fat 3 g), **carbohydrate** 14 g (of which sugars 5 g), **fibre** 4 g

✓✓	A, C
✓	B₁, calcium, potassium

1 Add the lemon juice to a bowl of cold water. Peel and slice the artichokes, adding them to the water as soon as they are cut. (Artichokes discolour quickly once peeled and exposed to air.)

2 Melt the butter in a large saucepan. Drain the artichokes and add them to the saucepan with the celery, onion, carrots and garlic. Cover the pan and sweat the vegetables gently for 10 minutes or until softened.

3 Stir in the stock and caraway seeds. Bring to the boil, then reduce the heat and cover the pan. Simmer for about 20 minutes or until the vegetables are tender. Cool the soup slightly, then purée it in a blender until smooth or press it through a fine sieve. Alternatively, use a hand-held blender to purée the soup in the pan.

4 Return the soup to the pan, if necessary. Stir in the milk and cream and season to taste with salt and pepper. Reheat the soup very gently without allowing it to boil. Meanwhile, cut the carrot for garnish into short, fine julienne or matchstick strips. Serve the soup hot, garnishing each portion with carrot strips and a little chopped parsley.

Some more ideas

• Use vegetable stock, preferably home-made rich (see page 23) instead of chicken stock.

• For celeriac and parsnip soup, use 500 g (1 lb 2 oz) peeled and chopped celeriac instead of Jerusalem artichokes, and 2 chopped parsnips instead of carrots. Omit the celery.

• Bacon is delicious with artichokes and other root vegetables. Cook 115 g (4 oz) rinded and chopped smoked back bacon in the butter, then remove with a draining spoon and set aside. Add the vegetables and continue as in the recipe. Sprinkle the bacon over the soup instead of carrot, together with wholemeal croutons (see page 21) and chopped parsley.

• For a substantial soup, spread a little mashed Stilton cheese on thick slices of French bread or ciabatta and toast until melted and bubbling, then float these in the soup just before serving.

Plus points

• Jerusalem artichokes are a useful winter vegetable. Combining them with familiar roots, such as carrots, is a good way of introducing them to children and bringing variety to the diet.

• Jerusalem artichokes contain compounds called fructoligosaccarides – a type of dietary fibre that stimulates friendly bacteria in the gut while inhibiting harmful bacteria.

Japanese miso soup

Shiitake mushrooms, ginger and a stock made with dried kombu seaweed bring rich savoury flavours to this Oriental broth, which is quick and easy to make. With delicate tofu and slightly peppery watercress, the resulting soup is ideal for a deliciously healthy first course before a stir-fry of mixed vegetables with noodles.

Serves 4

1 packet dried kombu seaweed, about 25 g

1 tbsp sake, Chinese rice wine or dry sherry

2 tsp caster sugar

½ tsp finely grated fresh root ginger

2 tbsp miso paste

4 spring onions, sliced at an angle

6 fresh shiitake mushrooms, thinly sliced

85 g (3 oz) tofu, diced

85 g (3 oz) watercress leaves

Preparation time: 10 minutes, plus 5 minutes soaking

Cooking time: about 20 minutes

1 Put the kombu seaweed in a saucepan and pour in 1 litre (1¾ pints) water. Bring slowly to the boil, then remove from the heat and cover the pan. Set aside for 5 minutes. Use a draining spoon to remove and discard the kombu seaweed.

2 Stir the sake, rice wine or sherry, sugar and ginger into the broth and bring back to the boil. Reduce the heat, and stir in the miso paste until it dissolves completely.

3 Add the spring onions, mushrooms, tofu and watercress. Cook very gently, stirring, for 2 minutes without allowing the soup to boil. Ladle the soup into small bowls and serve at once.

Plus points

● Research suggests that the humble soya bean is a powerhouse of disease-fighting ingredients. Soya beans and their products, such as tofu and miso paste, are rich in compounds called phytoestrogens. Growing evidence suggests that a diet rich in phytoestrogens can help to protect against heart disease, breast and prostate cancer, and osteoporosis (brittle bones). Eating soya products can also help to relieve many of the symptoms associated with the menopause.

Some more ideas

● The kombu seaweed can be finely shredded or snipped into fine strips with scissors and returned to the broth, if liked, to add an interesting texture contrast.

● For an intense herb flavour, add 2 tbsp chopped fresh coriander with the watercress.

● As a non-vegetarian alternative to dried kombu seaweed, use dashi stock powder to make the broth in step 1. Dashi is Japanese stock made from kombu seaweed and bonito flakes (dried fish). Alternatively, the rich vegetable stock on page 23 can be used as the base for the soup, giving a different but equally delicious result.

● This recipe can be used as the basis of Japanese udon noodle soup with chicken. Bring 1 litre (1¾ pints) chicken stock (preferably home-made, see page 24) to the boil. Stir in the sake and ginger and add 2 tbsp rich soy sauce. Omit the miso. In step 3 add 1 skinless boneless chicken breast (fillet), cut into very fine strips, and 1 packet udon noodles, about 215 g, with the spring onions and mushrooms. Omit the tofu and do not add the watercress at this stage. Bring to the boil, then simmer for 2 minutes or until the chicken strips are cooked. Then add the watercress and cook gently for 1 minute.

Each serving provides

kcal 55, protein 3 g, fat 2 g (of which saturated fat 0 g), carbohydrate 5.5 g (of which sugars 5 g), fibre 4 g

✓✓	calcium
✓	A, C, copper, iron

Golden lentil soup

This velvety-smooth soup owes its rich colour to a combination of lentils, parsnips and carrots. With dry sherry and a horseradish-flavoured cream adding to the flavour, it is a perfect dinner-party first course. Serve it with crunchy melba toast or oatcakes (if you want to make your own oatcakes, see the recipe on page 80).

Serves 6

30 g (1 oz) butter

1 large onion, finely chopped

450 g (1 lb) parsnips, cut into small cubes

340 g (12 oz) carrots, cut into small cubes

150 ml (5 fl oz) dry sherry

85 g (3 oz) red lentils

1.2 litres (2 pints) vegetable stock, preferably home-made light or rich (see page 23)

salt and pepper

fresh chives to garnish

To serve

2 tsp grated horseradish

6 tbsp crème fraîche

Preparation time: about 15 minutes

Cooking time: about 1¼ hours

Each serving provides

kcal 250, protein 6 g, fat 11 g (of which saturated fat 3 g), carbohydrate 25 g (of which sugars 11 g), fibre 6 g

✓✓✓	A
✓✓	B₁, B₆, folate, potassium
✓	calcium, iron

1 Melt the butter in a large saucepan. Add the onion, stir well and cover the pan. Sweat the onion over a gentle heat for 10 minutes or until softened. Stir in the parsnips, carrots and sherry. Bring to the boil, then cover the pan again and leave to simmer very gently for 40 minutes.

2 Add the lentils, stock, and salt and pepper to taste. Bring to the boil, then reduce the heat and cover the pan. Simmer for a further 15–20 minutes or until the lentils are tender. Purée the soup in a blender until smooth or use a hand-held blender to purée the soup in the pan. Return the soup to the pan if necessary, and reheat it gently until boiling. If it seems a bit thick, add a little stock or water.

3 Stir the grated horseradish into the crème fraîche. Snip some of the chives for the garnish and leave a few whole. Ladle the soup into warm bowls and top each portion with a spoonful of the horseradish cream. Scatter snipped chives over the top and add a few lengths of whole chive across the top of each bowl. Serve at once.

Some more ideas

• Use celeriac instead of parsnips, and swede instead of carrots. Prepare and cook the soup as in the main recipe. Dry white vermouth or white wine can be added in place of the sherry for a lighter flavour.

• For a lower-fat version, top each portion with 1 tsp creamed horseradish instead of the horseradish and crème fraîche mixture, and scatter chopped parsley over the soup.

Plus points

• Lentils are a good source of protein and an excellent source of fibre. High-fibre foods are bulky and make you feel full for longer, so are very satisfying. A diet high in fibre and low in fat is good for weight control.

• Root vegetables have long been enjoyed as an excellent source of vitamins and minerals during the winter months.

• Children who are reluctant to sample plain cooked vegetables will not even realise they are eating them in this tasty, colourful soup.

King prawn bisque

This classic seafood soup is ideal for a special first course. A last-minute addition of chopped red pepper brings a delightful flourish of flavour, texture and extra vitamins instead of the fat in the traditional swirl of cream.

Serves 6

450 g (1 lb) raw king prawns, without heads

4 tbsp dry white wine

4 slices of lemon

4 black peppercorns, lightly crushed

2 sprigs of parsley, stalks bruised

1 bulb of fennel

1 tsp lemon juice

15 g (½ oz) butter

1 tbsp sunflower oil

1 shallot, finely chopped

45 g (1½ oz) fine white breadcrumbs, made from day-old slices of bread

pinch of paprika

1 red pepper, seeded and finely diced

salt and pepper

chopped leaves from the fennel bulb, or herb fennel, to garnish

Preparation time: about 45 minutes, plus cooling

Cooking time: about 35 minutes

Each serving provides

kcal 165, **protein** 8 g, **fat** 6 g (of which saturated fat 2 g), **carbohydrate** 9 g (of which sugars 3 g), **fibre** 1 g

✓✓✓	A, B₆, B₁₂, C, phosphorus, selenium
✓✓	copper, iron, zinc
✓	B₂, folate, calcium, potassium

1 Peel the prawns and set them aside. Place the shells in a large saucepan. Pour in 1.2 litres (2 pints) cold water and add the white wine, lemon slices, peppercorns and parsley. Bring to the boil, then reduce the heat and simmer for 20 minutes. Skim off any scum that rises to the surface during cooking.

2 Use a small sharp knife to make a shallow slit along the curved back of each prawn. With the tip of the knife remove the black vein and discard it. Cover and chill the prawns until required.

3 Allow the prawn-shell stock to cool slightly, then pick out and discard the lemon slices. Line a sieve with muslin and place it over a large bowl or measuring jug. Process the stock in a blender or food processor until the shells are finely ground, then strain the stock through the muslin-lined sieve. Discard the residue from the shells.

4 Coarsely chop 85 g (3 oz) of the fennel, and finely chop the remainder of the bulb. Place the finely chopped fennel in a bowl, add the lemon juice and toss well, then cover closely with cling film and set aside.

5 Melt the butter with the oil in the rinsed-out saucepan. Add the coarsely chopped fennel and the shallot. Cook, stirring frequently, over a moderate heat for about 8 minutes or until the vegetables are soft but not browned. Stir in the breadcrumbs, paprika and stock. Bring slowly to the boil, then reduce the heat so that the soup simmers. Add the prawns and continue simmering for 3 minutes.

6 Use tongs or a draining spoon to remove 6 prawns for garnishing the soup. Set them aside. Season the soup with salt and pepper to taste and simmer for a further 15 minutes.

7 Purée the soup in a blender or food processor until smooth. Return to the pan and add the finely chopped fennel and the red pepper. Reheat the soup until piping hot. Serve garnished with the reserved prawns and chopped fennel leaves.

Plus points

• Prawns are a good source of low-fat protein. They are an excellent source of vitamin B₁₂, selenium and phosphorus.

• Making the stock with the prawn shells gives the bisque a full flavour, and at the same time boosts its calcium content.

Some more ideas

● To add extra fibre, sprinkle the soup with garlic-flavoured rye bread croutons just before serving. Cut 55 g (2 oz) light rye bread into 1 cm (½ in) cubes and toss these with 1 tbsp garlic-flavoured olive oil. Transfer to a baking tray and bake at 180°C (350°F, gas mark 4) for 10 minutes or until crisp.

● To serve the soup as a filling main course, make the stock with 1.3 litres (2¼ pints) water and add 250 g (8½ oz) frozen sweetcorn with the red pepper and fennel. Serve with a simple side salad of mixed leaves, cucumber and green pepper, and plenty of crusty bread

● A variety of other vegetables can be added with or instead of the red pepper. For example, try a mixture of small broccoli florets, finely chopped celery and frozen peas.

Simple seafood broth

Delicate seafood is complemented by saffron, tomatoes and courgettes in a clear and light, but well-flavoured, broth. The accompaniment, a piquant spread of creamy ricotta cheese and red pepper for French bread, is far lighter than classic rouille, the spicy mayonnaise traditionally served with seafood soups.

Serves 4

1 litre (1¾ pints) fish stock, preferably home-made (see page 24)

¼ tsp saffron threads

400 g (14 oz) mussels in shells, scrubbed

85 g (3 oz) peeled raw king prawns

85 g (3 oz) shelled scallops

85 g (3 oz) plaice fillet, skinned

2 tomatoes, skinned and diced

1 courgette, finely diced

salt and pepper

1 tbsp snipped fresh chives to garnish

Pepper spread

1 small red pepper, seeded and finely chopped

150 g (5½ oz) ricotta cheese

pinch of cayenne pepper, or to taste

1 small celery stick, finely chopped

1 tbsp snipped fresh chives

Preparation time: 40 minutes

Cooking time: 10 minutes

Each serving provides

kcal 310, **protein** 28 g, **fat** 7 g (of which saturated fat 3 g), **carbohydrate** 34 g (of which sugars 7 g), **fibre** 2 g

✓✓✓	C
✓✓	B₁, B₂, B₆, B₁₂, calcium, copper, selenium
✓	folate

1 First prepare the pepper spread. Stir the red pepper into the ricotta together with the cayenne pepper, celery, chives and salt to taste. Cover and chill until required.

2 Heat the fish stock in a large saucepan until boiling. Crumble the saffron into the stock and stir well, then remove from the heat and set aside.

3 To prepare the mussels, discard any broken shells or shells that do not close when tapped. Put the wet mussels into a clean saucepan and cover tightly. (There is no need to add water.) Cook over a moderate heat for 4 minutes, shaking the pan occasionally. Check that the mussels have opened – if not, cover and cook for a further 1–2 minutes.

4 Set a colander over the saucepan of stock and tip the mussels into it so that the juices from the shells are added to the stock. Leave the mussels until they are cool enough to handle, then remove them from their shells and set aside. Discard any unopened shells.

5 Use a small sharp knife to make a shallow slit along the back of each prawn. Use the tip of the knife to remove the black vein and discard it. Cut each scallop across into 2–3 thin slices, depending on size. Cut the plaice fillet into strips about 2 cm (¾ in) wide and 5 cm (2 in) long.

6 Reheat the fish stock until simmering. Add the mussels, prawns, scallops and strips of plaice. Stir, then heat until simmering gently again. Add the diced tomatoes and courgette with salt and pepper to taste. Simmer the soup for 3 minutes.

7 Ladle the soup into warm bowls and scatter chives over to garnish. Serve at once, with the pepper spread and lots of warm French bread.

Plus points

- Ricotta cheese is a useful source of calcium and protein, and it is considerably lower in fat than many other cheeses.
- The red pepper spread served with this broth is much lower in fat and richer in vitamin C and beta-carotene than the spicy mayonnaise rouille.

Some more ideas

• Use 100 g (3½ oz) cubed skinless salmon fillet instead of the mussels and sliced oyster mushrooms instead of the plaice fillet.

• For a poultry and pasta broth, use 300 g (10½ oz) skinless boneless chicken or turkey breasts (fillets), cut into fine strips, instead of the fish and seafood, and chicken stock (see page 24) instead of the fish stock. Heat the stock and saffron until boiling, then add 4 tbsp orzo pasta and the chicken or turkey. Simmer gently for 5–7 minutes or until the pasta is tender and the chicken or turkey is cooked and white in colour. Add the diced vegetables, bring back to the boil and serve.

• The red pepper spread makes an excellent dip for fresh raw vegetables such as celery, radishes, fennel or cucumber.

Chicken and potato chowder

The simple, delicious flavours of this soup will make it popular with all the family. Try it for lunch at the weekend, served with plenty of crusty bread and fresh fruit to follow.

Serves 4

1 tbsp extra virgin olive oil

2 lean smoked back bacon rashers, rinded and finely chopped

1 chicken thigh, about 140 g (5 oz), skinned

2 onions, finely chopped

500 g (1 lb 2 oz) potatoes, peeled and diced

750 ml (1¼ pints) chicken stock, preferably home-made (see page 24)

leaves from 4 sprigs of fresh thyme or ½ tsp dried thyme

300 ml (10 fl oz) semi-skimmed milk

salt and pepper

chopped parsley, or a mixture of chopped parsley and fresh thyme, to garnish

Preparation time: 20 minutes
Cooking time: about 50 minutes

Each serving provides

kcal 220, **protein** 12 g, **fat** 6 g (of which saturated fat 2 g), **carbohydrate** 30 g (of which sugars 9 g), **fibre** 2 g

✓✓ B₁, B₆, B₁₂, C, calcium, potassium

✓ B₂, niacin, copper, iron, zinc

1 Heat the oil in a large saucepan. Add the bacon, chicken and onions, and cook over a low heat for 3 minutes. Increase the heat and cook for a further 5 minutes, stirring the ingredients occasionally and turning the chicken once, until the chicken is pale golden.

2 Add the potatoes and cook for 2 minutes, stirring all the time. Pour in the stock, then add the thyme and seasoning to taste. Bring to the boil. Reduce the heat, cover the pan and leave to simmer for 30 minutes.

3 Using a draining spoon, transfer the chicken to a plate. Remove and chop the meat and discard the bone. Return the chicken to the soup. Stir in the milk and reheat the soup gently without boiling.

4 Ladle the soup into bowls and garnish with chopped parsley or parsley and thyme. Serve at once.

Some more ideas

● For a smooth result, purée the soup in a blender or food processor in step 3 after the chicken meat has been replaced.

● Garlic is delicious in potato soups – add 2–3 chopped garlic cloves with the potatoes. A pinch of grated nutmeg could also be stirred in with, or instead of, the thyme.

● For a winter vegetable soup use 800 g (1¾ lb) mixed diced leeks (white and pale green parts), carrot and swede instead of the onions and potatoes. Finely chop the green tops from the leeks, and add them to the soup with the milk at the end of cooking for extra colour.

● Boost the vitamin C and iron content with watercress. Add 75 g (2½ oz) watercress sprigs and the juice of 1 lemon with the chopped cooked chicken and purée the soup until smooth. Stir in the milk, adding an extra 150 ml (5 fl oz). Reheat the soup and serve, swirling 1 tbsp single cream in each bowl.

● Add 1 can chickpeas, butter beans or cannellini beans, about 400 g, drained, and halve the quantity of potatoes.

Plus points

● Potatoes undeservedly have a reputation for being fattening. In fact, they are rich in complex carbohydrate and low in fat, making them satisfying without being highly calorific. They also provide useful amounts of vitamin C and potassium, and good amounts of fibre.

● Onions contain a phytochemical called allicin, which is believed to help reduce the risk of cancer and also of blood clots forming, thereby helping to prevent coronary heart disease.

Zesty turkey broth

While lemon zest and parsley enliven this light turkey and vegetable soup, colourful carrots, celery and broccoli ensure that it is full of essential vitamins. The refreshing flavour stimulates the appetite, making the soup ideal for a first course. Chunks of Granary bread make a satisfying accompaniment.

Serves 4

1 lemon

15 g (½ oz) parsley

1 litre (1¾ pints) chicken stock, preferably home-made (see page 24)

2 carrots, cut into 1 cm (½ in) dice

2 celery sticks, cut into 1 cm (½ in) dice

225 g (8 oz) skinless turkey breast steaks, cut into 1 x 4 cm (½ x 1½ in) strips

100 g (3½ oz) small broccoli florets

salt and pepper

Preparation time: 15 minutes
Cooking time: about 20 minutes

Each serving provides

kcal 90, **protein** 14 g, **fat** 2 g (of which saturated fat 0.5 g), **carbohydrate** 5 g (of which sugars 4 g), fibre 2 g

✓✓✓	A, B$_6$, B$_{12}$, C
✓✓	potassium
✓	niacin, copper, folate, iron, selenium, zinc

1 Using a vegetable peeler, pare the zest off half the lemon in one long strip and place it in a large saucepan. Cut the thicker stalks off the parsley and tie them together in a neat bunch with fine string (they will contribute flavour to the soup). Add the bunch of parsley stalks to the pan. Set aside the rest of the lemon and parsley. Pour the stock into the pan and bring to the boil. Add the carrots and celery, reduce the heat, cover the pan and simmer for 5 minutes.

2 Add the turkey strips and reduce the heat, if necessary, so that the soup barely simmers. Cover and cook very gently for 5 minutes. Bring the soup back to the boil. Add the broccoli and cook, uncovered, for 3 minutes or until the broccoli is just tender.

3 Meanwhile, use a citrus zester to remove the remaining zest from the lemon in fine shreds. Alternatively, grate off the zest. Halve the lemon and squeeze its juice. Chop the reserved parsley. Remove the long strip of lemon zest and the bunch of parsley stalks from the soup. Stir in the lemon juice with most of the shreds of zest and most of the chopped parsley. Season the soup to taste.

4 Ladle the soup into warm soup bowls. Garnish with the remaining lemon zest and parsley and serve hot.

Plus points

● As well as being extremely low in fat, this soup is full of vitamins and disease-fighting phytochemicals.

● Broccoli provides beta-carotene along with vitamin C and several of the B vitamins. Adding it towards the end of cooking minimises the vitamin losses caused by prolonged heating.

● Carrots may not really help you see in the dark but they are one of the richest sources of the antioxidant beta-carotene, which helps to protect against cancer.

Some more ideas

● Noodles can be added to make a more substantial soup. Start with 1.2 litres (2 pints) stock. In step 2, once the soup has been brought back to the boil, add 85 g (3 oz) thin or medium egg noodles, breaking them up as you drop them in. Boil for 1 minute, then add the broccoli. Alternatively, add broken up spaghetti with the carrots and celery.

● Use skinless boneless chicken, lean pork or beef instead of the turkey and vary the vegetables. For example, try 100 g (3½ oz) leek or fennel instead of celery and add a few chopped spring onions or snipped fresh chives with the parsley.

light soups

● For a Thai-style soup, use lime instead of lemon and coriander instead of parsley. Tear 3 lime leaves in half and tie in a square of muslin with 1 stalk of lemongrass, cut into 3, 1 small halved and seeded fresh red chilli, a few thick coriander stalks, 1 halved garlic clove and a 2.5 cm (1 in) piece fresh root ginger, cut into 4. Add this sachet of aromatics to the stock in step 1, and remove it at the beginning of step 4. Instead of broccoli, add 100 g (3½ oz) mange-tout, each one cut into 3 long strips. Add 1–2 tbsp fish sauce, to taste, with the lime juice. If you like hot Thai food, seed and finely chop a second small fresh red chilli and add it with the lime zest and coriander.

Herb-scented ham and pea soup

A hint of cream makes this fresh green soup seem delightfully indulgent. The high proportion of peas fills the soup with vitamins and fibre, while a modest amount of lean cooked ham adds protein and depth of flavour. Serve with crusty bread for a satisfying starter or add a sandwich and enjoy it for lunch.

Serves 4

1 tbsp extra virgin olive oil

1 onion, chopped

1 small carrot, diced

2 garlic cloves, sliced

1 leek, chopped

1 celery stick, diced

2 tbsp chopped parsley

1 potato, peeled and diced

100 g (3½ oz) lean boiled or baked ham, diced

500 g (1 lb 2 oz) shelled fresh or frozen peas

½ tsp dried herbes de Provence, or to taste

1 litre (1¾ pints) vegetable stock, preferably home-made light (see page 23), or a mixture of half stock and half water

3 large lettuce leaves, finely shredded

2 tbsp whipping cream

salt and pepper

Preparation time: about 15 minutes

Cooking time: about 1 hour

1 Heat the oil in a saucepan. Add the onion, carrot, garlic, leek, celery, parsley, potato and ham. Stir well, then cover the pan, reduce the heat and sweat the vegetables for about 30 minutes or until they are softened. Stir the vegetables occasionally so that they cook evenly.

2 Add the peas, herbes de Provence and stock, or stock and water. Bring to the boil, then reduce the heat to moderately-high and cook until the peas are just tender – allow about 10 minutes for fresh peas or 5 minutes for frozen. Add the lettuce and cook gently for a further 5 minutes.

3 Purée half to two-thirds of the soup in a blender, then stir the purée back into the rest of the soup. Alternatively, use a hand-held blender to partly purée the soup in the pan. Reheat the soup gently, if necessary, and taste and adjust the seasoning. Ladle the soup into warm bowls. Swirl a little cream into each portion and serve at once.

Plus points

- Throughout history garlic has been used to treat everything from athlete's foot to colds and flu. Scientific facts now give credence to the folklore – for example, allicin, the compound that gives garlic its characteristic smell and taste, is known to act as a powerful antibiotic and it also has anti-viral and anti-fungal properties.

- Peas are a good source of the B vitamins B_1 B_6, and niacin, and they provide useful amounts of folate and vitamin C. As a good source of soluble fibre, they are useful for anyone with high cholesterol levels.

Some more ideas

- For a more substantial soup, add a generous spoonful of freshly cooked rice or vermicelli or creamy mashed potatoes to each bowl.

- For a split pea soup, use 140 g (5 oz) dried split peas (yellow or green) instead of fresh or frozen peas. Add 125 g (4½ oz) peeled, diced celeriac, ¼ tsp ground cumin and a few shakes of chilli sauce, such as Tabasco, to the vegetables and ham in step 1. Increase the volume of stock to 1.5 litres (2¾ pints), and simmer for 1–1½ hours or until the peas are tender. Omit the lettuce and whipping cream. Purée all the soup until smooth. Add salt and pepper to taste and reheat.

Each serving provides

kcal 250, **protein** 16 g, **fat** 8 g (of which saturated fat 3 g), **carbohydrate** 30 g (of which sugars 7 g), **fibre** 8 g

✓✓✓	A, B_1, B_6, C, folate
✓✓	iron, potassium, zinc
✓	niacin, calcium, copper

light soups

44

Classic gazpacho

This traditional Spanish soup is full of wonderfully fresh flavours and packed with vitamins as all the vegetables are raw. Cool and refreshing, it is the ideal choice for a simple lunch or mid-summer supper, with some crusty country-style bread or rolls. Or serve it as a light starter on a warm evening.

Serves 4

500 g (1 lb 2 oz) full-flavoured tomatoes, quartered and seeded

¼ cucumber, peeled and coarsely chopped

1 red pepper, seeded and coarsely chopped

2 garlic cloves

1 small onion, quartered

1 slice of bread, about 30 g (1 oz), torn into pieces

2 tbsp red wine vinegar

½ tsp salt

2 tbsp extra virgin olive oil

500 ml (17 fl oz) tomato juice

1 tbsp tomato purée

To serve

1 red pepper

4 spring onions

¼ cucumber

2 slices of bread, made into croutons (see page 21)

Preparation time: 20 minutes, plus 2 hours chilling

Each serving provides Ⓥ

kcal 215, **protein** 6 g, **fat** 9 g (of which saturated fat 1.5 g), **carbohydrate** 30 g (of which sugars 17 g), **fibre** 5 g

✓✓✓ A, B₁, B₆, C, niacin, potassium

---

1 Mix all the ingredients in a large bowl. Ladle batches of the mixture into a blender and purée until smooth. Pour the soup into a large clean bowl, cover and chill for 2 hours.

2 Prepare the vegetables to serve with the soup towards the end of the chilling time. Seed and finely dice the red pepper; thinly slice the spring onions; and finely dice the cucumber. Place these vegetables and the croutons in separate serving dishes.

3 Taste the soup and adjust the seasoning, then ladle it into bowls. Serve at once, offering the accompaniments so that they can be added to taste as the soup is eaten.

Some more ideas

• For a milder flavour, use 2 shallots instead of the small onion.

• In very hot weather, add a few ice cubes to the soup just before serving, to keep it well chilled. This will also slightly dilute it.

• To make a fresh green soup, use 500 g (1 lb 2 oz) courgettes instead of tomatoes and cucumber. Add 450 ml (15 fl oz) vegetable stock, preferably home-made (see page 23), instead of the tomato juice. Use a green pepper instead of a red one. Add 15 g (½ oz) fresh basil leaves and 85 g (3 oz) pitted green olives. Mix, purée and chill the soup as above. Serve with a diced green pepper instead of red.

Plus points

• Up to 70% of the water-soluble vitamins – B and C – can be lost in cooking. In this classic soup the vegetables are eaten raw, which means they retain maximum levels of vitamins and minerals.

• Peppers have a naturally waxy skin that helps to protect them against oxidation and prevents loss of vitamin C during storage. As a result their vitamin C content remains high even several weeks after harvesting.

light soups

Fresh fruit soup

Not only is this refreshing soup perfect on sweltering summer days, it could also give you a vitamin boost in winter when you feel slightly under the weather. Stirred up from a variety of delicious raw fruit and vegetables, it is an easy way to top up on protective nutrients. Serve it as a high-vitality starter or snack.

Serves 4

500 ml (17 fl oz) pineapple juice
500 ml (17 fl oz) orange juice
½ cucumber, diced
¼ red onion, finely chopped
1 small red pepper, seeded and chopped
½ fresh red chilli pepper, seeded and
   chopped
juice of 1 lime
½ tsp caster sugar
1 large mango
10 cape gooseberries
1 firm pear
2 passion fruit
1 tbsp chopped fresh mint
2 tsp chopped fresh coriander
sprigs of fresh mint to garnish (optional)

Preparation time: 30 minutes, plus 1 hour
   chilling

Each serving provides   Ⓥ
kcal 150, protein 2 g, fat 0.5 g (of which
saturated fat 0 g), carbohydrate 37 g (of
which sugars 36 g), fibre 2.5 g

✓✓✓ A, B₁, B₆, C
✓✓ folate, potassium

1 Mix together the pineapple and orange juices in a large bowl. Add the cucumber, onion, pepper, chilli, lime juice and sugar, and stir well to mix. Cover and chill for 1 hour so that the flavours can mix and develop.

2 Peel, stone and dice the mango, and add to the soup. Discard the papery skins from the cape gooseberries, then quarter the fruit. Core and dice the pear and add to the soup with the cape gooseberries. Cut the passion fruit in half, scoop out the flesh with a teaspoon and stir into the soup with the chopped mint and coriander.

3 Ladle the soup into bowls and garnish with mint sprigs, if liked, then serve at once.

Some more ideas

● Make the soup as spicy as you like by adding more chopped fresh chilli – ½ chilli gives only the slightest of kicks.
● For a slightly thicker soup, purée the cucumber, onion, pepper and chilli together in a blender or food processor until smooth, then add to the fruit juices in step 1.
● In place of the mango, cape gooseberries, pear and passion fruit, use 1 peeled and diced kiwi fruit, 1 peeled and diced guava (or drained and diced canned guava) or 1 stoned and diced peach, ¼ peeled and diced pineapple and 1 diced banana.

● If you happen to come across jícama, a juicy root vegetable from America's southwest and Mexico, it is a delicious, crunchy ingredient to add to the soup. Peel and dice it, then add it with the fruit just before serving.
● Whizz the soup in a blender or food processor to make a high-vitamin refreshing drink for any time of year.

Plus points

● The World Cancer Research Fund suggests that eating 5 or more portions of fruit and vegetables a day could prevent 20% of all cases of cancer. This soup is a great way to help you meet the 5-a-day target.
● Studies into the incidence of bowel cancer within different population groups suggest that people who eat more fruit and vegetables are less likely to get this disease.
● Research at Harvard University found that drinking 1 glass of orange juice daily could reduce the risk of stroke by 25%.

Iced melon and berry soup

Almost any variety of green-fleshed melon, such as Galia or Honeydew, can be used for this very pretty soup, but it is essential that the melon be perfectly ripe and sweet. Serve the soup as a refreshing first course when the weather is hot, dressing up each bowlful with a swirl of berry purée and some whole berries.

Serves 4

1 large ripe green-fleshed melon, about 1.25 kg (2¾ lb)
juice of 1 lime
3.5 cm (1½ in) piece fresh root ginger, peeled and grated
150 g (5½ oz) blueberries
120 ml (4 fl oz) freshly squeezed orange juice
2 tbsp Greek-style yogurt
150 g (5½ oz) raspberries or strawberries
salt

Preparation time: 20 minutes, plus 30 minutes chilling

1 Halve the melon, discard the seeds and scoop the flesh out of the peel into a blender or food processor. Add the lime juice and ginger. Purée until smooth, stopping occasionally to push the pieces of melon to the bottom of the goblet or bowl. Pour the purée into a bowl, cover and chill for 30 minutes or until cold.

2 Put the blueberries into the blender or food processor. Add the orange juice and yogurt and purée until smooth. Transfer to a second bowl, cover and chill for about 30 minutes or until cold.

3 Divide the melon soup among 4 chilled shallow glass bowls or dishes. Spoon a quarter of the blueberry purée onto the centre of each in a decorative pattern. Scatter the raspberries or strawberries on top. Serve at once.

Some more ideas

- Try orange-fleshed melon, such as Ogen, Charentais or Cantaloupe, and top the soup with sliced kiwi fruit instead of the red berries.
- Use 2 kg (4½ lb) watermelon instead of the green melon. Chop the flesh, discarding the seeds, then purée with the lime juice and 1 seeded and chopped fresh green chilli instead of the ginger. Coarsely crush the blueberries with the raspberries and/or strawberries, adding 1–2 tbsp orange juice. Omit the yogurt.

Plus points

- All melons provide vitamins B and C, and are very low in calories. Their high water content makes them a delicious and refreshing thirst-quencher.
- Ginger is thought to be an anti-inflammatory agent that can help ease some of the symptoms of arthritis.
- Blueberries are rich in vitamin C and a useful source of soluble fibre. They also contain several phytochemicals: athocyanosides which help to fight infection and inflammation, flavonoids which strengthen blood capillaries and improve circulation, and ellagic acid which can help to prevent cell damage that can lead to cancer. Like cranberries, blueberries also contain a natural antibiotic that can help to prevent urinary tract infections.

Each serving provides (V)

kcal 110, **protein** 3 g, **fat** 1 g (of which saturated fat 0.5 g), **carbohydrate** 24 g (of which sugars 24 g), **fibre** 4 g

✓✓✓	C
✓✓	potassium
✓	B_1, B_2, calcium, folate

Soups that Make a Meal

Substantial soups that are full of goodness

Ladle out healthy eating with these irresistible hearty soups, ideal for mid-week suppers and weekend lunches. Bright green broccoli and watercress soup with salmon cakes is a treat to share with friends, and everyone will want seconds of pumpkin soup with rosemary-scented muffins. A chilli-spiced turkey and bean soup with a refreshing salsa and warm tortillas will tempt all the family, as will a lightly curried mulligatawny. Enjoy borscht as never before, or go Oriental with fragrant rice-coated meatballs in a vegetable-packed broth.

Spinach and onion soup with tomato crostini

A colourful vegetarian version of classic French onion soup, this makes a filling lunch or supper. The secret of the rich flavour lies in frying the onions very slowly until they are well browned, caramelised and sweet.

Serves 4

30 g (1 oz) butter

1 tbsp extra virgin olive oil

500 g (1 lb 2 oz) large onions, thinly sliced

1 tsp caster sugar

2 garlic cloves, chopped

1 litre (1¾ pints) vegetable stock, preferably
   home-made rich (see page 23)

115 g (4 oz) broccoli, finely chopped

115 g (4 oz) spinach leaves, torn

salt and pepper

Tomato crostini

8 thick slices of French bread

1 garlic clove, halved

2 tsp tomato purée

2 tomatoes, each cut into 8 wedges

30 g (1 oz) Parmesan cheese, freshly grated

Preparation time: 30 minutes

Cooking time: about 1 hour

Each serving provides   Ⓥ

kcal 420, **protein** 13 g, **fat** 15 g (of which
saturated fat 6 g), **carbohydrate** 63 g (of
which sugars 14 g), **fibre** 5 g

✓✓	A, C
✓	B₁, B₆, B₁₂, E, folate

1 Melt the butter with the oil in a large saucepan. Add the onions and fry gently for 10 minutes, stirring occasionally, until softened and pale golden. Stir in the sugar and garlic, then continue to fry for 10 minutes, stirring occasionally, until the onions are browned and caramelised.

2 Stir in the stock and a little seasoning, and bring to the boil. Reduce the heat, cover the pan and simmer for 30 minutes. Add the broccoli and simmer for a further 3 minutes. Take the pan off the heat and stir in the spinach, then cover and leave to stand while making the tomato crostini.

3 Preheat the grill to high, and lightly toast the slices of bread on both sides. Rub one side of each slice with the cut garlic clove and spread lightly with tomato purée. Add 2 tomato wedges to each slice, season with salt and pepper and sprinkle the Parmesan cheese over the top. Grill for about 2 minutes or until the cheese melts and is just bubbling.

4 While the crostini are grilling, reheat the soup, if necessary. Ladle into 4 warm bowls. Float 2 tomato crostini in each bowl of soup and serve immediately.

Some more ideas

• For a pepper and onion soup, replace the spinach and broccoli with 1 red and 1 orange pepper, both seeded and thinly sliced. Add the peppers with the onions in step 1. Just before serving, stir in 200 g (7 oz) skinned and diced tomatoes and some torn fresh basil leaves.

• Use 55 g (2 oz) crumbled feta cheese instead of the Parmesan on the crostini. Drizzle a little extra virgin olive oil over the cheese and tomatoes before grilling them.

Plus points

• Spinach is a good source of several antioxidants including vitamins C and E, and carotenoid compounds. It also provides useful amounts of niacin and vitamin B₆, and is a good source of folate.

• Although spinach is traditionally thought of as a good source of iron, only 2–5% of the iron can be used by the body. This is due to oxalic acid in the spinach, which binds the iron, making most of it unavailable. Eating spinach with something that provides vitamin C, such as the tomatoes here, makes more of the iron available.

• Broccoli is a good source of folate, which is vital for women planning a baby or during the first 3 months of pregnancy.

Minestrone

This minestrone makes the most of winter vegetables, and is full of vitamin goodness. Beans and pasta make it even more nourishing. Serve with chunks of fresh country-style bread for a satisfying meal.

Serves 6

1 tbsp extra virgin olive oil

1 large onion, finely chopped

3–4 garlic cloves, finely chopped

200 g (7 oz) dried cannellini or borlotti beans, soaked overnight and drained

1 can plum tomatoes in juice, about 400 g

2 tbsp tomato purée

200 g (7 oz) carrots, finely diced

150 g (5½ oz) swede, finely diced

150 g (5½ oz) celeriac, finely diced

250 g (8½ oz) peeled pumpkin flesh, finely diced

1 tsp fresh thyme leaves

1 bay leaf

3 allspice berries, finely crushed

200 g (7 oz) potatoes, peeled and finely diced

150 g (5½ oz) green beans, cut into short lengths

100 g (3½ oz) small pasta shapes, such as farfallini (bows) or conchigliette (shells), or broken-up spaghetti

125 g (4½ oz) spinach, chopped

4 tbsp shredded fresh basil

salt and pepper

55 g (2 oz) Parmesan cheese, freshly grated, to serve

Preparation time: 30 minutes, plus overnight soaking

Cooking time: about 1½ hours

1 Heat the oil in a large saucepan. Add the onion and garlic, cover and cook for 4–5 minutes, stirring occasionally, until the onion is translucent. Add the cannellini or borlotti beans and pour in 2 litres (3½ pints) water. Bring to the boil and boil for 10 minutes, then reduce the heat, cover the pan and simmer for 30 minutes.

2 Add the tomatoes with their juice, breaking them up with a fork, then add the tomato purée, carrots, swede, celeriac and pumpkin. Stir in the thyme, bay leaf and crushed allspice. Bring back to simmering point, then cover the pan again and simmer for 20 minutes.

3 Stir in the potatoes and green beans. Continue simmering, covered, for 15 minutes. Stir in the pasta and cook, still covered, for a further 10 minutes or until the cannellini or borlotti beans are tender and the pasta is cooked.

4 Add the spinach and basil, and season to taste with salt and pepper. Simmer uncovered for 2–3 minutes until the spinach has wilted. Ladle the soup into warm bowls and serve at once, with the Parmesan cheese to sprinkle on top.

Some more ideas

• Butternut squash or any other type of squash can be used instead of the pumpkin.

• Add 100 g (3½ oz) rinded and chopped lean smoked back bacon with the onion and garlic in step 1. Alternatively, crisp-fried Parma ham can be sprinkled over the soup when serving.

Plus points

• Beans and pulses are an excellent source of soluble fibre. Unfortunately they can produce unpleasant side effects such as wind and bloating. To prevent this, be sure to cook them thoroughly – undercooked beans are difficult to digest and thus more likely to cause wind.

• Pasta scores healthily low on the Glycaemic Index, which means that it breaks down slowly into glucose and glycogen in the body, providing long-lasting energy.

Each serving provides ⓥ

kcal 290, **protein** 16 g, **fat** 6 g (of which saturated fat 2 g), **carbohydrate** 45 g (of which sugars 9 g), **fibre** 9 g

✓✓	A, C, folate
✓	B_1, B_6, B_{12}, E, niacin

soups that make a meal

Borscht with crunchy mash

Guaranteed to beat off the winter blues, this hearty beetroot soup is served with creamy mashed potatoes enlivened with crunchy raw vegetables. There are as many types of borscht as there are cooks in Eastern Europe. The soup is often strained and served as a clear broth, but this puréed version retains every gram of goodness.

Serves 4

1 tbsp extra virgin olive oil

1 onion, chopped

1 large carrot

½ tsp lemon juice

1 bulb of fennel

500 g (1 lb 2 oz) raw beetroot

1 litre (1¾ pints) vegetable stock, preferably home-made light or rich (see page 23)

800 g (1¾ lb) floury potatoes, peeled and cut into small cubes

120 ml (4 fl oz) semi-skimmed milk

4 tbsp Greek-style yogurt

2 spring onions, finely chopped

salt and pepper

chopped leaves from the fennel bulb, herb fennel or parsley to garnish

Preparation time: about 35 minutes

Cooking time: about 50 minutes

Each serving provides Ⓥ

kcal 300, **protein** 11 g, **fat** 4 g (of which saturated fat 1 g), **carbohydrate** 56 g (of which sugars 21 g), **fibre** 7 g

✓✓✓	A, folate
✓✓	B₁, B₆, C
✓	iron

1 Place the oil in a large saucepan and add the onion. Set aside 55 g (2 oz) of the carrot for the mash, then chop the rest and add it to the pan. Mix well, cover and cook over a moderate heat for 5 minutes to soften the onion.

2 Place the lemon juice in a small bowl. Cut the bulb of fennel into quarters. Finely grate one quarter into the lemon juice and toss well. Finely grate the reserved carrot and add it to the grated fennel. Cover and set aside.

3 Chop the remaining fennel and add to the saucepan. Peel and dice the beetroot, and add it to the pan. Pour in the stock and bring to the boil. Reduce the heat, cover the pan and simmer for about 30 minutes or until all the vegetables are tender.

4 Meanwhile, bring another pan of water to the boil. Add the potatoes and boil for 10 minutes or until very tender. Drain the potatoes well and return them to the pan. Place over a low heat for about 1 minute to dry, shaking the pan occasionally to prevent the potatoes from sticking. Remove from the heat and set aside, covered to keep hot.

5 Purée the soup in a blender or food processor until smooth, or purée in the pan using a hand blender. Return the soup to the pan, if necessary, and reheat. Taste and adjust the seasoning.

6 While the soup is reheating, set the pan of potatoes over a moderate heat and mash until completely smooth, gradually working in the milk. Stir in the yogurt, grated fennel and carrot, spring onions and seasoning to taste.

7 Divide the mashed potato among 4 bowls, piling it up in the centre. Ladle the soup around the mash and sprinkle with chopped fennel or parsley. Serve at once.

Plus points

• Beetroot is a particularly rich source of the B vitamin folate, which may help to protect against heart disease and spina bifida. It also provides useful amounts of iron. The characteristic deep red colour comes from a compound called betacyanin, which has been shown to prevent the growth of tumours in animal studies.

• Adding grated raw vegetables to mashed potatoes is a good way of including them in a hot meal, especially for children.

• Fennel contains phytoestrogen, a naturally occurring plant hormone that encourages the body to excrete excess oestrogen. A high level of oestrogen is associated with increased risk of breast cancer. Fennel also contains useful amounts of folate.

soups that make a meal

Some more ideas

● Other delicious raw vegetable additions to mashed potatoes are finely chopped celery, grated celeriac, finely shredded red or Savoy cabbage, shredded Brussels sprouts and coarsely chopped spring onions. They all contribute extra vitamins and minerals.

● Serve the borscht chunky instead of puréed, and add 2 tbsp hazelnut oil to the mashed potatoes instead of the yogurt.

● Instead of spooning the borscht around a pile of mash, garnish each bowl of soup simply with 1 tbsp Greek-style yogurt, soured cream or creamed horseradish, then sprinkle with chopped fresh fennel or parsley.

Pumpkin soup with muffins

Pumpkin blends to a richly coloured, ultra-smooth soup, here enhanced by the wonderful flavour of rosemary. Crunchy hazelnut, pumpkin and rosemary muffins complement the soup perfectly.

Serves 4

1 tbsp extra virgin olive oil

1 onion, finely chopped

500 g (1 lb 2 oz) peeled pumpkin flesh, diced, about 675 g (1½ lb) unpeeled weight

1 potato, peeled and diced

2 garlic cloves, chopped

1 tbsp chopped fresh rosemary

900 ml (1½ pints) vegetable stock, preferably home-made light (see page 23)

150 ml (5 fl oz) semi-skimmed milk

100 g (3½ oz) fromage frais

salt and pepper

Rosemary and hazelnut muffins

100 g (3½ oz) hazelnuts, roughly chopped and toasted

340 g (12 oz) self-raising flour

2 tsp baking powder

85 g (3 oz) butter, melted

2 tbsp chopped fresh rosemary

2 eggs, beaten

200 ml (7 fl oz) semi-skimmed milk

To garnish

100 g (3½ oz) fromage frais

a little paprika

4 sprigs of fresh rosemary

Preparation time: 35 minutes

Cooking time: about 1 hour

1 Heat the oil in a large saucepan. Add the onion and cook over a moderate heat for 5 minutes until softened. Add the pumpkin and cook for 4–5 minutes or until softened but not browned. Use a draining spoon to remove 100 g (3½ oz) of the fried onion and pumpkin mixture and reserve it for the muffins.

2 Add the potato, garlic and rosemary to the pan. Cook for 2 minutes, stirring occasionally, then pour in the stock and add seasoning to taste. Bring to the boil. Reduce the heat, cover the pan and leave to simmer for 30 minutes.

3 Meanwhile, make the muffins. Preheat the oven to 220ºC (425ºF, gas mark 7). Finely chop the reserved fried pumpkin and onion, then place in a bowl. Add the hazelnuts, flour, baking powder, butter, chopped rosemary, eggs and milk. Use a fork to mix the ingredients together until evenly combined.

4 Place 12 deep paper muffin cases in a muffin tray with cups 5 cm (2 in) in diameter and 3 cm (1¼ in) deep. Divide the mixture among the cases. Bake for 12–15 minutes or until risen, golden and cracked across the top. Remove the muffins from the tray and wrap them in a clean tea-towel to keep them warm.

5 Purée the soup in a blender or food processor until smooth, or purée in the pan using a hand-held blender. Return the soup to the pan, if necessary, and stir in the milk and fromage frais. Reheat gently but do not boil. Taste and adjust the seasoning.

6 Ladle the soup into warm bowls. Garnish with fromage frais, paprika and sprigs of rosemary, and serve with the warm muffins.

Plus points

• As well as being an excellent source of beta-carotene, pumpkin also provides several other antioxidants including lutein and zeaxanthin. These are believed to help protect against age-related macular degeneration (AMD), an eye disease that affects 20% of people over the age of 65 and is the leading cause of blindness in the western world.

• Hazelnuts are a rich source of vitamins B_1, E and niacin. They also provide useful amounts of calcium, iron and zinc, and are a good source of the essential fatty acids.

soups that make a meal

Another idea
• For a spicy pumpkin and sweet potato soup, use peeled and diced sweet potato instead of ordinary potato. Add 1 tsp coarsely crushed cumin seeds, 2 tsp coarsely crushed coriander seeds and a 2.5 cm (1 in) piece of fresh root ginger, peeled and finely chopped, with the garlic instead of the rosemary. Just before serving, add a dash of chilli sauce, such as Tabasco, for a hint of chilli heat. Garnish the soup with fromage frais, a sprinkle of ground cumin and chopped fresh coriander.

Each serving provides

kcal 860, **protein** 25 g, **fat** 46 g (of which saturated fat 17 g), **carbohydrate** 91 g (of which sugars 14 g), **fibre** 7 g

✓✓✓	B_1, E
✓✓	A, B_2, B_6, niacin, calcium, potassium, zinc
✓	C, folate, iron

Chunky mulligatawny

This lightly spiced soup is robust and satisfying – the perfect choice for a simple meal on a cold day. Generous spoonfuls of cool, crunchy fresh raita bring a terrific contrast in flavour and texture to the soup, which is finished with fried curried onion. Naan or pitta bread mop up both soup and raita.

Serves 4

1 litre (1¾ pints) vegetable stock, preferably home-made light or rich (see page 23)

1 onion, chopped

2 carrots, cut into 1 cm (½ in) dice

2 celery sticks, cut into 1 cm (½ in) dice

1 parsnip, cut into 1 cm (½ in) dice

2 potatoes, peeled and cut into 1 cm (½ in) dice

50 g (1¾ oz) chestnut mushrooms, sliced

1 garlic clove, chopped

2 large sprigs of fresh coriander, chopped

salt and pepper

4 plain naan breads or 4–8 pitta breads, to serve

Curried onion

1 tbsp sunflower oil

1 onion, thinly sliced

1 garlic clove, crushed

1 tbsp mild curry paste

Apple and courgette raita

1 small courgette

7.5 cm (3 in) piece cucumber

1 dessert apple

150 g (5½ oz) plain low-fat yogurt

2 tbsp chopped parsley

handful of fresh mint leaves

Preparation time: 25 minutes
Cooking time: about 45 minutes

1 Bring the stock to the boil in a large saucepan. Add the onion, carrots, celery, parsnip, potatoes, mushrooms and garlic. Bring back to the boil, then reduce the heat and cover the pan. Simmer for 30 minutes. The vegetables should be soft and break up when squashed against the side of the pan with a fork.

2 Meanwhile, prepare the curried onion. Heat the oil in a small frying pan, add the onion and cook over a moderate heat, stirring occasionally, for 10–12 minutes or until the onion softens and begins to caramelise. Add the garlic and fry for a further 1–2 minutes. Stir in the curry paste and 1 tbsp water, then cook, stirring, for 2–3 more minutes. Remove from the heat and set aside.

3 To make the raita, grate the courgette and cucumber into a bowl. Core and grate the apple and add to the courgette and cucumber. Lightly stir in the yogurt and parsley. Tear the mint leaves or coarsely shred them with scissors and fold them into the raita. Add seasoning to taste. Transfer to a serving bowl and set aside.

4 Purée about half of the soup in a blender or food processor until just smooth, then pour it back into the soup in the pan. Alternatively, use a hand-held blender to coarsely purée the soup in the pan, leaving some vegetables diced. Reheat the soup and taste for seasoning. If the soup is slightly too thick, add a little boiling water to thin it to your liking.

5 Lightly stir in the curried onion and chopped fresh coriander, then ladle the soup into warm bowls. Serve at once, offering the raita separately, to be added to the soup in large spoonfuls or eaten with the naan bread or pitta as an accompaniment.

Plus points

• Yogurt is a good source of vitamins B_2 and B_{12}, and the minerals calcium and phosphorus.

• Antibiotics, stress and poor diet can easily upset the balance of good and bad bacteria in the gut. Eating yogurt ensures a regular supply of good bacteria and prevents the growth of the bad bacteria that can cause thrush and candida. There is also some evidence to suggest that the good bacteria help to strengthen the immune system.

soups that make a meal

Another idea

- For a smooth, dhal-style soup, add 100 g (3½ oz) yellow split peas with the vegetables in step 1, leaving out the parsnip and potatoes. Use only 900 ml (1½ pints) stock. Also add 1 can chopped tomatoes, about 400 g, with the juice, 1 heaped tsp cumin seeds, 1 heaped tsp roasted and ground coriander seeds, 1 fresh red chilli, seeded and chopped, and ½ tsp turmeric. Bring to the boil, then reduce the heat and cover the pan. Simmer for 1 hour. Purée all of the soup until fairly smooth, then reheat it gently before stirring in the curried onion and fresh coriander.

Each serving provides

kcal 585, **protein** 14 g, **fat** 27 g (of which saturated fat 3 g), **carbohydrate** 75 g (of which sugars 13 g), **fibre** 5 g

✓✓	A, B₁
✓	B₂, B₁₂, C, folate, calcium, phosphorus

Broccoli soup with salmon cakes

Salmon goes so well with broccoli and watercress, both in flavour and colour.
Here the fish is combined with potato and dill in miniature cakes that are delicious
served in the fresh green vegetable soup.

Serves 4

30 g (1 oz) butter

1 potato, peeled and cubed

300 g (10½ oz) broccoli, coarsely chopped

1 large leek, sliced

115 g (4 oz) watercress

1 litre (1¾ pints) vegetable stock, preferably
   home-made light (see page 23)

salt and pepper

Salmon cakes

700 g (1 lb 9 oz) potatoes, peeled and cubed

300 g (10½ oz) salmon fillet

200 ml (7 fl oz) semi-skimmed milk

3 spring onions, finely chopped

2 tbsp chopped fresh dill

grated zest of 1 lemon

55 g (2 oz) semolina

3 tbsp sunflower oil

To garnish

watercress leaves

finely shredded lemon zest

Preparation and cooking time: about 1¼ hours

Each serving provides

kcal 500, **protein** 28 g, **fat** 25 g (of which
saturated fat 7 g), **carbohydrate** 56 g (of
which sugars 6 g), **fibre** 6 g

✓✓✓	A, B₁,C
✓✓	B₆, B₁₂, E, folate, niacin
✓	D, selenium

1 First make the salmon cakes. Add the potatoes to a pan of boiling water and cook for 10–12 minutes or until tender. Drain well and mash thoroughly until smooth.

2 While the potatoes are cooking, place the salmon in a deep-sided frying pan. Add the milk and heat until barely simmering, then cover the pan and simmer gently for 3–4 minutes or until the salmon flakes easily. Use a draining spoon to lift the salmon from the milk. Reserve the milk. Flake the salmon, discarding any bones and skin, then add it to the mashed potatoes. Mix in the spring onions, dill, lemon zest and seasoning to taste.

3 Place the semolina on a large plate. Shape the salmon mixture into 20 small balls, the size of golf balls, then flatten them into neat patties, coating them lightly on both sides with semolina as they are shaped. Cover and set aside in the refrigerator.

4 To make the soup, melt the butter in a large saucepan. Add the potato, broccoli and leek and cook gently for about 10 minutes or until softened. Stir in the watercress. Add the stock and bring to the boil, then reduce the heat and cover the pan. Simmer for about 10 minutes or until the vegetables are just tender. Cool the soup slightly, then purée it in a blender or food processor

until smooth. Return the soup to the pan. Stir in the milk used to cook the fish and seasoning to taste. Reheat gently until simmering.

5 Cook the salmon cakes while the soup is reheating. Heat half the oil in a large frying pan and cook half of the cakes for 3–4 minutes on each side or until golden. Drain on kitchen paper. Heat the remaining oil and cook the remaining cakes.

6 Ladle the soup into warm bowls and float 2–3 salmon cakes in each one. Garnish with watercress and lemon zest, and serve with the remaining salmon cakes.

Plus points

● Salmon is an oily fish and a good source of omega-3 fatty acids, which help to protect against heart disease. It also provides B-group vitamins and vitamins A and D.

● Semolina, milled from wheat grain, is a starchy carbohydrate that also provides some protein as well as minerals.

soups that make a meal

Some more ideas

● Use 1 can salmon, about 200 g, drained, to make the salmon cakes. Add 200 ml (7 fl oz) semi-skimmed milk when reheating the soup.

● For a vegetarian version, make sweetcorn and Parmesan cheese patties instead of fishcakes. Add 1 can sweetcorn, about 200 g, drained, to the potato mixture instead of the salmon. Omit the lemon and dill, and add 3 tbsp freshly grated Parmesan cheese and ½ tsp Tabasco or other hot pepper sauce. Shape and cook the patties as for the salmon cakes. Stir in 200 ml (7 fl oz) semi-skimmed milk when reheating the soup.

● For a homely, chunky soup, instead of making cakes, add both quantities of potatoes to the soup. Cut the salmon into small cubes and add to the soup in step 4 for the last 5 minutes of simmering. Do not purée the soup. Stir in 200 ml (7 fl oz) semi-skimmed milk and heat through before serving.

Fish soup with pepper polenta

Good stock provides the flavour base for this delicate broth. When home-made stock is not available, try one of the high-quality commercial stocks sold chilled rather than a stock cube. The polenta accompaniment is prepared in advance, so the soup is simple to cook at the last minute – ideal when friends come to lunch.

Serves 4

900 ml (1½ pints) fish stock, preferably home-made (see page 24)

1 bay leaf

1 sprig of parsley

1 sprig of fresh thyme

2 celery sticks, thinly sliced

1 bulb of fennel, quartered lengthways and thinly sliced

2 carrots, halved lengthways and thinly sliced

zest of 1 lemon, finely shredded or coarsely grated

1 shallot, finely chopped

1 garlic clove, finely chopped

1 fresh red chilli, halved and seeded (optional)

225 g (8 oz) monkfish fillet, cut into bite-sized chunks

225 g (8 oz) skinless white fish fillet, such as cod or haddock, cut into bite-sized chunks

salt and pepper

leaves from the fennel bulb, herb fennel or fresh dill to garnish

Pepper polenta sticks

2 red peppers, halved lengthways and seeded

1 tsp salt

200 g (7 oz) instant polenta

45 g (1½ oz) Parmesan cheese, freshly grated

Preparation and cooking time: about 1½ hours, plus about 1½ hours cooling and 10–20 minutes infusing

1 Prepare the polenta sticks in advance. Preheat the grill to high. Place the pepper halves on the grill rack, cut sides down, and grill for 10 minutes or until the skin is charred all over. To make them easy to peel, transfer them to a polythene bag and leave to stand for 15 minutes or until cool enough to handle. Peel the peppers and cut lengthways into 5 mm (¼ in) wide strips. Set aside.

2 Cook the polenta with the salt according to the instructions on the packet. Continue to cook, stirring constantly, until it is thick.

3 Sprinkle a plastic chopping board or tray with water and turn the polenta out onto it. Use a wet palette knife to spread out the polenta into a rectangle about 1 cm (½ in) thick. Arrange the strips of pepper diagonally on top, gently pressing them into the polenta. Wet a sharp knife and use this to trim and neaten the edges of the polenta rectangle. Leave to cool.

4 Preheat the oven to 200°C (400°F, gas mark 6) and grease a baking tray. Sprinkle the Parmesan cheese over the polenta rectangle and cut it into 16 sticks. Transfer the polenta sticks to the baking tray and bake for 15 minutes or until the cheese is melted and bubbling. Leave to cool

for 2 minutes, then transfer to a wire rack and leave to cool completely.

5 For the soup, pour the stock into a saucepan. Tie the bay leaf, parsley and thyme together into a bouquet garni and add to the pan with celery, fennel, carrots, lemon zest, shallot, garlic and chilli, if using. Heat gently until boiling, then simmer for 5 minutes or until the vegetables are slightly tender. Cover the pan and remove it from the heat. Leave to stand for 10–20 minutes so the flavours can infuse the liquid.

6 Remove and discard the bouquet garni and chilli halves. Bring the liquid back to the boil. Reduce the heat, add the monkfish and white fish, and poach for about 4 minutes or until all the fish chunks are opaque and will flake easily. Season with salt and pepper to taste.

7 Transfer the polenta sticks to a serving plate. Ladle the soup into warmed bowls and sprinkle with the fennel leaves or dill. Serve at once.

soups that make a meal

Each serving provides

kcal 370, **protein** 29 g, **fat** 6 g (of which saturated fat 2 g), **carbohydrate** 47 g (of which sugars 10 g), **fibre** 5 g

✓✓✓	A, C
✓✓	B₁₂, folate, potassium
✓	B₁, selenium

Another idea

● To make mushroom polenta, cook 170 g (6 oz) sliced mushrooms with 1 crushed garlic clove and 1 tbsp chopped shallot in 1 tbsp extra virgin olive oil for about 5 minutes. Add 1 tbsp snipped fresh chives and spread over the polenta sticks. Sprinkle 2 tbsp freshly grated Parmesan cheese over the mushrooms and brown under the grill instead of baking.

Plus points

● Celery and fennel provide potassium. Celery also acts as a diuretic, helping to reduce fluid and salt retention.

● Like other white fish, cod, haddock and monkfish are very low in fat and calories.

Piquant cod chowder

A variety of vegetables ensures that this wonderful soup is as healthy as it is delicious. The broth can be prepared a day in advance, ready for adding the fish at the last minute, which is useful when cooking mid-week meals. Planning ahead like this means a healthy dinner can be on the table in minutes.

Serves 4

2 sprigs of parsley

2 sprigs of fresh thyme

1 bay leaf

7.5 cm (3 in) piece of celery stick

1 can chopped tomatoes, about 400 g

750 ml (1¼ pints) fish stock,
   preferably home-made (see page 24)

4 tbsp medium cider

1 large onion, chopped

400 g (14 oz) waxy potatoes, cut into large
   chunks

225 g (8 oz) carrots, thickly sliced

225 g (8 oz) courgettes, thickly sliced

225 g (8 oz) green beans, cut into short
   lengths

1 yellow or red pepper, seeded and sliced

550 g (1¼ lb) cod fillet, skinned and cut into
   large pieces

salt and pepper

To garnish

2 tbsp finely chopped parsley

1 tbsp snipped fresh chives

finely shredded zest of 1 lemon

Preparation time: about 20 minutes
Cooking time: about 40 minutes

1 Tie the parsley, thyme and bay leaf with the celery to make a bouquet garni. Put the bouquet garni in a large saucepan. Add the tomatoes and their juice, the stock, cider and onion, stir and bring to the boil. Reduce the heat to low, half cover the pan and simmer for 15 minutes.

2 Add the potatoes and carrots. Increase the heat to moderate and cook, covered, for 15 minutes or until the vegetables are almost tender. Stir in the courgettes, green beans and yellow or red pepper and continue simmering, covered, for 5 minutes or until all the vegetables are tender. Discard the bouquet garni.

3 Season with salt and pepper to taste, then add the cod to the gently simmering broth. Cover and cook gently for 3–5 minutes or until the fish is opaque, just firm and flakes easily. Do not allow the broth to boil rapidly or the fish will overcook and start to break up.

4 For the garnish, mix the parsley, chives and lemon zest together. Ladle the fish and vegetables into warm bowls, then add the broth. Sprinkle the garnish over the top and serve at once.

Some more ideas

• Ring the changes by using different vegetables – broccoli florets, sliced leeks, sweetcorn, peas and green peppers are all suitable. Add them instead of the courgettes, green beans and yellow pepper in step 2.

• Smoked haddock is delicious in this dish, on its own or replacing half of the white fish.

Plus points

• Serving wholemeal rolls with the soup will add to the dietary fibre provided by all the vegetables.

• Green beans are a good source of fibre and they also provide valuable amounts of folate.

• Courgettes provide niacin and vitamin B_6.

Each serving provides

kcal 290, **protein** 33 g, **fat** 2.5 g (of which saturated fat 0.5 g), **carbohydrate** 35 g (of which sugars 16 g), **fibre** 7 g

✓✓✓	B_6, B_{12}, C
✓✓	A, folate, iron, potassium
✓	B_1, niacin, calcium, selenium

soups that make a meal

Hearty mussel soup

This soup tastes fabulous. The diced potatoes absorb the flavours from the herbs and vegetables to make a mellow complement to the mussels. Warm soda bread is an ideal partner, delicious for dunking and mopping up the last of the soup. To complete the meal, serve a light, fruity dessert for a refreshing, vitamin-packed finale.

Serves 4

1 kg (2¼ lb) mussels in shells, scrubbed

2 tbsp extra virgin olive oil

1 onion, finely chopped

2 garlic cloves, finely chopped

2 leeks, thinly sliced

3 celery sticks, thinly sliced

2 carrots, diced

400 g (14 oz) potatoes, peeled and cut into small cubes

900 ml (1½ pints) vegetable stock, preferably home-made light (see page 23)

150 ml (5 fl oz) dry white wine

1 tbsp lemon juice

1 bay leaf

1 sprig of fresh thyme

4 tbsp chopped parsley

2 tbsp snipped fresh chives

salt and pepper

Preparation time: 30 minutes

Cooking time: 40–50 minutes

Each serving provides

kcal 260, protein 17 g, fat 8 g (of which saturated fat 1 g), carbohydrate 24 g (of which sugars 7 g), fibre 4.5 g

✓✓✓	A
✓✓	B_6, B_{12}, C, folate
✓	B_1, B_2, selenium

1 Prepare and cook the mussels following the instructions in step 3 of Simple seafood broth (see page 38). Drain the mussels, reserving the juices that have come from the shells. Reserve a few mussels in their shells for garnish; remove the remainder from their shells and set aside. Discard the shells and any unopened mussels.

2 Heat the oil in the rinsed-out saucepan. Add the onion, garlic, leeks, celery and carrots, and cook gently for 5–10 minutes, stirring frequently, until the vegetables are softened but not browned. Add the potatoes, stock, wine, reserved juices from the mussels, lemon juice, bay leaf, thyme and salt and pepper to taste. Bring to the boil, then reduce the heat to low. Cover the pan and simmer the soup gently for 20–30 minutes or until all the vegetables are tender.

3 Remove the bay leaf and thyme, then add the shelled mussels, parsley and chives to the pan. Heat gently for about 1 minute. Do not allow the soup to boil or cook for any longer than this or the mussels will become tough and shrink.

4 Ladle the soup into warm bowls and garnish with the reserved mussels in shells. Serve at once, while piping hot.

Another idea

• Cooked fresh mussels are available in most supermarkets, usually vacuum packed and displayed in chiller cabinets. Use 300 g (10½ oz) shelled weight of mussels. Alternatively, use 2 cans mussels in brine, each about 250 g, or 4 cans smoked mussels in vegetable oil, each about 85 g. Drain the canned mussels thoroughly and pat dry before adding them to the soup.

Plus points

• Like other shellfish, mussels are a good low-fat source of protein. They are an extremely good source of vitamin B_{12} and provide useful amounts of copper, iodine, iron, phosphorus and zinc.

• Vitamin C from the potatoes, parsley and chives aids the absorption of iron from the mussels.

• Celery is said to have a calming effect on the nerves.

Turkey chilli soup with salsa

This colourful soup is inspired by the spicy and complex flavours of chilli con carne. Full of delicious vegetables and served with tortillas and a refreshing salsa, it makes a healthy main course that is fun to eat.

soups that make a meal

Serves 6

2 tsp extra virgin olive oil

450 g (1 lb) minced turkey

1 onion, finely chopped

2 celery sticks, finely chopped

1 red or yellow pepper, seeded and finely chopped

3 garlic cloves, finely chopped

1 can chopped tomatoes, about 400 g

1 litre (1¾ pints) turkey or chicken stock, preferably home-made (see page 24)

¼ tsp ground coriander

¼ tsp ground cumin

¼ tsp dried oregano

½ tsp chilli powder, or to taste

200 g (7 oz) courgettes, diced

150 g (5½ oz) fresh or frozen sweetcorn, thawed if necessary

1 can borlotti or kidney beans, about 400 g, drained and rinsed

salt and pepper

12 flour tortillas to serve (1 packet, about 312 g)

Avocado salsa

2 tbsp fresh lime juice

2 avocados

100 g (3½ oz) cherry tomatoes, quartered

6 spring onions, finely chopped

50 g (1¾ oz) rocket, chopped

Preparation time: 35 minutes
Cooking time: 50 minutes

1 Heat the oil in a large saucepan over a high heat. Add the turkey and cook for about 4 minutes, stirring occasionally, until lightly browned. Reduce the heat to moderate and add the onion, celery, pepper and garlic. Continue cooking, stirring frequently, for about 2 minutes or until the onion begins to soften. Stir in the tomatoes with the juice from the can, the stock, coriander, cumin, oregano and chilli powder. Bring to the boil, then reduce the heat to low, cover the pan and simmer for 20 minutes.

2 Preheat the oven to 160°C (325°F, gas mark 3). Add the courgettes, sweetcorn and borlotti or kidney beans to the soup. Bring back to the boil, then reduce the heat to low and cover the pan again. Simmer the soup for a further 10 minutes or until the courgettes are just tender.

3 Meanwhile, wrap the stack of tortillas tightly in foil and heat in the oven for about 10 minutes or until warmed through and soft.

4 To make the salsa, place the lime juice in a bowl. Halve, stone, peel and dice the avocados, then add to the bowl and toss them in the lime juice. Gently mix in the tomatoes, spring onions and rocket, adding seasoning to taste. Take care not to break up the diced avocados.

5 Season the soup with salt and pepper to taste. Ladle the soup into warm bowls and serve. The salsa can either be spooned on top of the soup or eaten as an accompaniment wrapped in the warm tortillas.

Plus points

- Beans and pulses are a good source of dietary fibre, particularly soluble fibre which can help to reduce high blood cholesterol levels. They also provide useful amounts of vitamin B_1 and iron.
- Vitamin C from the salsa will help the body absorb iron from the beans.
- Avocados are rich in vitamin B_6, which is vital for making the 'feel-good' hormone serotonin. They also provide the antioxidant vitamin E which can help to protect against heart disease.

Each serving provides

kcal 400, **protein** 28 g, **fat** 11 g (of which saturated fat 2 g), **carbohydrate** 51 g (of which sugars 10 g), **fibre** 8 g

✓✓✓	A, C
✓✓	B_1, B_2, B_6, B_{12}
✓	E, folate, niacin, iron, selenium

Another idea

● For a vegetarian chilli bean soup, omit the turkey and replace the chicken stock with vegetable stock (preferably home-made rich, see page 23). Thickly slice 1 aubergine and brush the slices very lightly on both sides with extra virgin olive oil. Lightly brown the aubergine slices on both sides in a non-stick frying pan over a moderately high heat, or under the grill. Remove the aubergine from the pan or grill and cut into cubes, then add to the soup with the tomatoes, stock and spices.

Lamb and barley soup

Full of tender lamb cubes, deliciously nutty pearl barley and chunky vegetables, this substantial soup is really a meal in a bowl. Savoury herb-scented scones are served alongside.

Serves 4

1 tbsp extra virgin olive oil

340 g (12 oz) lean boneless lamb, cut into 2 cm (¾ in) dice

1 onion, chopped

2 carrots, cut into 1 cm (½ in) dice

250 g (8½ oz) turnips, cut into 1 cm (½ in) dice

250 g (8½ oz) swede, cut into 1 cm (½ in) dice

100 g (3½ oz) pearl barley

1.2 litres (2 pints) lamb or chicken stock, preferably home-made (see pages 24–25)

2 tsp chopped fresh rosemary

1 tsp chopped fresh thyme

100 g (3½ oz) frozen peas

salt and pepper

Herb scones

225 g (8 oz) plain flour

1 tbsp baking powder

55 g (2 oz) butter

3 tbsp chopped parsley

3 tbsp snipped fresh chives

1 tbsp finely chopped fresh rosemary

150 ml (5 fl oz) semi-skimmed milk

Preparation time: 20 minutes

Cooking time: about 1¼ hours

1 Heat the oil in a large saucepan and fry the lamb over a high heat for about 5 minutes or until browned, stirring frequently. Use a draining spoon to transfer the lamb to a plate. Add the onion, carrots, turnips and swede to the oil remaining in the pan. Stir well and cook for 2–3 minutes or until the vegetables are starting to soften.

2 Return the lamb to the saucepan and stir in the pearl barley, stock, rosemary and thyme with seasoning to taste. Heat until simmering, then reduce the heat and cover the pan. Simmer gently for 40 minutes.

3 Meanwhile, make the scones. Preheat the oven to 230°C (450°F, gas mark 8) and grease a baking tray. Sift the flour and baking powder into a bowl. With your fingertips, rub in the butter until the mixture resembles fine breadcrumbs. Stir in the parsley, chives and rosemary, then make a well in the middle and pour in all but about 1 tbsp of the milk. Gradually mix the dry ingredients into the milk to make a fairly soft dough.

4 Turn the scone dough out onto a well-floured surface. Dust your hands with a little flour, then lightly pat and knead the dough into a smooth ball. Flatten the dough and roll it out into a round about 2.5 cm (1 in) thick and 13 cm (5½ in) across.

5 Place the dough round on the baking tray and use a large sharp knife to cut it into 8 wedges, leaving them in place. Wipe the knife with a damp cloth between cuts to prevent the dough from sticking to it. Brush with the reserved milk and bake immediately for 10–15 minutes or until well risen and deep golden brown on top. Slide the scone round onto a wire rack to cool.

6 Add the peas to the soup and simmer for a further 10 minutes. Taste for seasoning, then ladle the soup into large bowls and serve with the scones. If you like, wrap the scone round loosely in a folded napkin or clean tea-towel and take it to the table on a large flat basket or board. Break it into wedges to serve.

Plus points

• Pearl barley contains traces of gluten and is therefore unsuitable for anyone following a gluten-free diet, but it is useful for those on wheat-free diets. Although highly refined, weight for weight pearl barley provides more fibre than brown rice.

• Unlike the majority of vegetables, which are most nutritious when eaten raw, carrots are a better source of beta-carotene when they are cooked.

Some more ideas

• For a lamb and split pea soup, replace the pearl barley with 55 g (2 oz) split yellow peas. Instead of the onion and turnips, use 3 sliced leeks and 250 g (8½ oz) diced celeriac.

• Rather than scones you can cook small dumplings in the soup. To make them, mix 85 g (3 oz) self-raising flour with 30 g (1 oz) vegetable suet, 1 tbsp chopped parsley and 1 tbsp snipped fresh chives. Bind together into a dough with 4 tbsp cold water and roll into a sausage shape on a floured surface. Cut into 8 equal portions and roll each into a ball. Add to the simmering soup with the peas in step 7.

Each serving provides

kcal 640, **protein** 31 g, **fat** 24 g (of which saturated fat 12 g), **carbohydrate** 78 g (of which sugars 10 g), **fibre** 7 g

✓✓✓	A
✓✓	B_1, B_2, B_6, B_{12}, iron
✓	C, calcium

Oriental meatball broth

Aromatic rice and pork meatballs and lots of interesting vegetables bring Oriental flavours to this satisfying main-meal soup. Serve it at the table in a warmed tureen or straight from the pan.

Serves 4

225 g (8 oz) red chard leaves

1.4 litres (2½ pints) chicken stock, preferably home-made (see page 24)

2.5 cm (1 in) piece fresh root ginger, peeled and cut into thin strips

3 tbsp dry sherry

2 tbsp light soy sauce, or to taste

200 g (7 oz) baby corn, each sliced diagonally into 2–3 pieces

115 g (4 oz) shiitake mushrooms, thinly sliced

200 g (7 oz) mange-tout, each cut diagonally into 2–3 pieces

1 can sliced bamboo shoots, about 220 g, drained

6 spring onions, thinly sliced diagonally

Rice and pork meatballs

170 g (6 oz) long-grain rice

340 g (12 oz) lean minced pork

2.5 cm (1 in) piece fresh root ginger, peeled and grated

6 spring onions, chopped

1 garlic clove, finely chopped

2 tbsp soy sauce

½ tsp toasted sesame oil

½ tsp five-spice powder

pinch of chilli powder

225 g (8 oz) pak choy

Preparation time: 20 minutes

Cooking time: about 40 minutes

1 First prepare the meatballs. Place the rice in a saucepan and pour in plenty of water to cover, then bring to the boil. Boil for 1 minute, then drain the rice in a sieve and leave to cool.

2 Mix the pork with the ginger, spring onions, garlic, soy sauce, sesame oil, five-spice powder and chilli powder. Strip the green leaves of the pak choy off the thick white stalks. Finely chop the leaves and add them to the pork. Reserve the stalks for the broth. Pound the mixture with a spoon until thoroughly combined.

3 Turn the drained rice into a large shallow bowl and separate the grains with a fork. Rinse your hands, then take a small lump of pork mixture, squeeze it together and roll it into a small ball about the size of a walnut. Roll the meatball in the rice, pressing it into the grains to coat it thickly. Press the rice firmly onto the meatball and set aside on a plate or dish. Shape the remaining pork mixture to make about 20 rice meatballs.

4 Cover the bottom of a steamer rack with a single layer of red chard, leaving gaps between the leaves. (If using stacking bamboo steamer baskets, you will need 2.) Add the meatballs in one layer, leaving space between them for the rice to swell. Bring the stock and ginger to the boil in the steamer base.

Set the steamer on top and cover. Steam the meatballs for 35 minutes.

5 While the meatballs are cooking, cut the stalks of the pak choy across into 1 cm (½ in) pieces. Remove the steamer from the pan and set it aside on a plate. Add the sherry, soy sauce, baby corn, shiitake mushrooms, mange-tout, remaining red chard leaves, bamboo shoots and spring onions to the stock. Bring back to the boil, then replace the steamer rack and steam for a further 5 minutes.

6 Carefully transfer the rice and pork balls to a warm serving bowl. Add the chard leaves from the steamer to the broth. Taste the broth and add more soy sauce, if liked, then transfer it to a warm tureen. To serve, ladle some broth and vegetables into 4 warm bowls and add a few rice and pork meatballs to each. Ladle in more broth and add meatballs during the meal as required.

Each serving provides

kcal 430, **protein** 32 g, **fat** 10 g (of which saturated fat 3 g), **carbohydrate** 51 g (of which sugars 7 g), **fibre** 6 g

✓✓ A, B$_1$, B$_2$, B$_6$, B$_{12}$, C, folate, niacin, potassium

soups that make a meal

Another idea

• Instead of steaming the rice and pork balls they can be poached gently in the stock for 20 minutes, then the vegetables can be added and the broth finished as in the main recipe. The rice tends to make the broth slightly cloudy, but the result tastes just as delicious.

Plus points

• Shiitake mushrooms contain lentinan, which is believed to help strengthen the immune system. These tasty mushrooms are also thought to help protect against cancer.

• Pork is a good source of vitamin B_1 and a useful source of several of the other B vitamins.

• Green leafy vegetables are good sources of vitamin C, folate and beta-carotene.

Venison soup with currant relish

This soup has an excellent meaty flavour, rather like traditional oxtail soup but made with leaner venison. The deliciously piquant and fruity blackcurrant relish perfectly complements the rich soup.

Serves 6

2 tbsp extra virgin olive oil

1 large onion, finely chopped

1 garlic clove, crushed

300 g (10½ oz) minced venison

8 juniper berries, crushed

90 ml (3 fl oz) red wine

140 g (5 oz) potato, peeled and diced

200 g (7 oz) celeriac, diced, weighed when peeled

150 g (5½ oz) swede, diced, weighed when peeled

125 g (4½ oz) carrot, diced

1 litre (1¾ pints) beef stock, preferably home-made (see page 25)

salt and pepper

chopped parsley or fresh coriander to garnish

24 oatcakes (1 packet, about 250 g)

Blackcurrant relish

1 tbsp extra virgin olive oil

3 large shallots, each cut into 8 wedges

16 juniper berries, crushed

3 tbsp caster sugar

1 tbsp red wine vinegar

150 g (5½ oz) fresh or frozen blackcurrants

Preparation time: 55 minutes

Cooking time: about 1 hour

1 Heat the oil in a large saucepan and add the onion and garlic. Cook for 10 minutes, stirring occasionally, until the onion has softened and is starting to brown.

2 Add the venison and juniper berries and cook over a high heat for about 5 minutes, stirring and breaking up the meat, until it has browned. Stir in the red wine, potato, celeriac, swede, carrot, stock and seasoning to taste. Bring to the boil, then reduce the heat and cover the pan. Simmer the soup gently for 30 minutes.

3 Meanwhile, make the blackcurrant relish. Heat the oil in a small saucepan and add the shallots. Cook, stirring occasionally, for about 5 minutes or until the shallots have softened. Stir in the juniper berries, sugar, vinegar and 4 tbsp water, then boil rapidly for 5–7 minutes or until well reduced. Stir in the blackcurrants and cook for a further 2–4 minutes or until the mixture forms a pulpy relish. Leave to cool.

4 Purée the soup in a food processor or blender. Return it to the pan and reheat gently. Ladle the soup into warm bowls and top each portion with a spoonful of blackcurrant relish. Scatter chopped parsley or coriander over the top and serve with oatcakes and the remaining relish.

Some more ideas

● For a pork and cider soup, use lean minced pork instead of venison and medium-dry cider instead of red wine. Omit the juniper berries and add 1 tsp chopped fresh sage.

● For a refreshingly tart apple relish, use 150 g (5½ oz) peeled, diced cooking apples instead of blackcurrants and 4 tbsp cider instead of water. Add 1 tsp chopped fresh sage instead of the juniper berries and reduce the quantity of sugar to 2 tbsp.

Plus points

● Venison is exceptionally low in fat compared to other meat – 1.1 g fat per 100 g (3½ oz). The same weight of beef contains 4.6 g fat and chicken 4.3 g fat.

● Blackcurrant skins contain anthocyanins, a phytochemical that is anti-inflammatory and inhibits the growth of bacteria such as *E. coli* in the gut.

Each serving provides

kcal 390, **protein** 18 g, **fat** 13 g (of which saturated fat 1 g), **carbohydrate** 47 g (of which sugars 16 g), **fibre** 4 g

✓✓✓	C, potassium
✓✓	A, B₁, B₆, copper, iron, zinc
✓	B₂, selenium

soups that make a meal

78

Rabbit soup with herb oatcakes

A wholesome meal-in-a-bowl, this soup is similar to Scotch broth, but made with lean diced rabbit rather than lamb. Aromatic tarragon and a mixture of vegetables give the soup a fabulous flavour, and an accompaniment of Scottish-style oatcakes brings a contrasting texture to complete the meal.

Serves 4

2 tbsp extra virgin olive oil

1 onion, coarsely chopped

2 celery sticks, chopped

1 large leek, sliced

2 carrots, thickly sliced

400 g (14 oz) lean boneless rabbit, diced

1.2 litres (2 pints) chicken stock, preferably home-made (see page 24)

2 tsp red wine vinegar

1 tbsp redcurrant jelly

1 tbsp chopped fresh tarragon or 1 tsp dried tarragon

115 g (4 oz) mixed long-grain and wild rice

115 g (4 oz) green beans, cut into short lengths, or frozen cut green beans

salt and pepper

Tarragon oatcakes

225 g (8 oz) medium oatmeal

1 tbsp chopped fresh tarragon or 1 tsp dried tarragon

¼ tsp salt

¼ tsp baking powder

30 g (1 oz) butter, melted

Preparation time: 40 minutes
Cooking time: about 1¼ hours

1 Heat the oil in a large heavy-based saucepan. Add the onion, celery, leek and carrots, and cook gently for 5 minutes or until the onion and leek begin to soften. Stir in the rabbit and continue to cook, stirring occasionally, for 2–3 minutes.

2 Pour in the stock and vinegar, then stir in the redcurrant jelly and tarragon with salt and pepper to taste. Bring to the boil. Reduce the heat, cover and simmer for 30 minutes.

3 Meanwhile, make the oatcakes. Preheat the oven to 160°C (325°F, gas mark 3). Place the oatmeal in a bowl and stir in the tarragon, salt and baking powder. Add 4 tbsp boiling water to the melted butter, then stir into the oatmeal to make a fairly stiff paste.

4 Sprinkle a baking tray with flour. Gently roll the oatmeal dough into a ball and place it on the baking tray. Press or roll it out into a round measuring about 23 cm (9 in) in diameter. The dough is very crumbly at this stage, so press any cracks together with your fingertips. (The oatcakes firm up during baking.) Press the edge of the dough round to neaten it and cut into 8 wedges with a sharp knife. Bake for 30 minutes or until lightly browned. Carefully transfer the cooked oatcakes to a wire rack to cool.

5 Stir the rice into the soup and continue simmering, covered, for a further 15 minutes or until the rice is tender. Add the green beans and bring back to simmering point, then cook, uncovered, for a final 5 minutes or until the beans are tender.

6 Taste the soup and adjust the seasoning, if necessary. Ladle into warm bowls and serve at once, with the warm oatcakes.

Plus points

● Rabbit is a very low-fat meat and it has plenty of flavour.

● Oats and oatmeal are a good source of soluble fibre. This can help to reduce high blood cholesterol levels and slow the absorption of sugar in the body, keeping blood sugar levels stable.

Each serving provides

kcal 610, **protein** 33 g, **fat** 21 g (of which saturated fat 6 g), **carbohydrate** 74 g (of which sugars 8 g), **fibre** 7 g

✓✓	A, B_1, B_{12}, folate, niacin, copper, iron, zinc
✓	B_2

soups that make a meal

Some more ideas

• To make a hearty rabbit casserole, replace the diced rabbit with 4 rabbit joints. Cook in a flameproof casserole, browning the joints with the vegetables in step 1. Omit the vinegar and replace half the stock with red wine. Omit the rice. Cover and cook gently on the hob or in the oven at 160°C (325°F, gas mark 3) for 1½ hours or until the rabbit is tender. Add the green beans for the last 10 minutes of cooking. Serve with baked potatoes or mixed long-grain and wild rice.

• For a vegetarian variation, omit the rabbit and use vegetable stock. Use 2 leeks and add 1 crushed garlic clove with the vegetables in step 1. In step 5, add 225 g (8 oz) frozen broad beans with the rice, and 225 g (8 oz) shredded Savoy cabbage with the green beans.

Quick Soups and Casseroles

Great dishes in less than 30 minutes

Soups and casseroles can be just right for a quick bite.
Raid the storecupboard to bring exotic flavours and
simple goodness to a variety of meals. Make a tasty
chowder with canned kippers and sweetcorn, or enjoy the
goodness of frozen vegetables in a luscious Garden of
Eden soup. Fresh wild mushrooms and aromatic fennel
make an elegant starter soup. A Malay-inspired casserole
of spicy fish in coconut milk is
perfect to round off a lazy summer
day, while in winter a warming
goulash of pork and red cabbage is
fast and fabulous.

Garden of Eden soup

An assortment of vegetables cooked in tomato juice and stock makes a simple, satisfying soup that tastes terrific. For this recipe you can take advantage of frozen vegetables, such as broccoli, beans and peas. They cut down on preparation time, and are just as nutritious as fresh vegetables.

Serves 4

300 ml (10 fl oz) boiling water

1 vegetable stock cube, crumbled, or 2 tsp vegetable bouillon powder or paste

1 litre (1¾ pints) tomato juice

2 garlic cloves, crushed

4 spring onions, finely chopped

1 large potato, scrubbed and diced

1 large carrot, diced

100 g (3½ oz) frozen broccoli florets

100 g (3½ oz) white cabbage, finely shredded or coarsely chopped

55 g (2 oz) frozen cut green beans

55 g (2 oz) frozen peas

55 g (2 oz) frozen broad beans

8 large sprigs of fresh basil

salt and pepper

Preparation time: 10 minutes

Cooking time: about 20 minutes

1 Pour the boiling water into a saucepan. Stir in the stock cube, powder or paste, the tomato juice, garlic, spring onions, potato and carrot. Bring to the boil, then reduce the heat and cover the pan. Simmer the soup for about 10 minutes, stirring occasionally.

2 Use a sharp knife to cut any large frozen broccoli florets into smaller pieces, then add them to the soup with the cabbage, green beans, peas and broad beans. Bring the soup back to the boil, then reduce the heat slightly, but keep the soup simmering rapidly. Cook for about 5 minutes or until the vegetables are just tender but still crisp.

3 Taste and season the soup, then ladle it into warm bowls. Use scissors to snip half the basil into shreds and scatter over the soup, discarding the tough ends of the sprigs. Add a whole sprig of basil to each portion and serve at once.

Some more ideas

● Instead of weighing out 4 types of frozen vegetables, use 250 g (8½ oz) frozen mixed vegetables. There are many different mixtures for simmering or stir-frying and all are great for making quick soups.

● For a hearty soup, add 1 can borlotti beans, about 400 g, drained and rinsed, with the frozen vegetables. Before serving, swirl 1 tsp pesto into each bowl of soup and sprinkle with 1 tsp lightly toasted pine nuts.

● The soup can be varied according to the fresh or frozen vegetables you have in the house. For example, try 1 peeled sweet potato with, or instead of, the ordinary potato and add 1 peeled and diced turnip for a hearty root-vegetable soup.

Plus points

● This is a good example of a 'cold-start' recipe, in which the vegetables are added straight to the liquid without being cooked in fat. The resulting soup is virtually fat free.

● Different fruit and vegetables contain different phytochemicals, so it is important to eat a variety. This soup includes a good mixture of vegetables.

Each serving provides Ⓥ

kcal 135, **protein** 7 g, **fat** 1 g (of which saturated fat 0 g), **carbohydrate** 25 g (of which sugars 14 g), **fibre** 6 g

✓✓✓	A, C
✓✓	B₆
✓	iron

Wild mushroom broth with herby ciabatta croutons

Mixtures of fresh wild mushrooms, widely available in supermarkets, are good for making a quick soup that tastes really special. Instead of thickening or puréeing the soup, serving it as a light broth allows the individual flavours of the mushrooms, vegetables and herbs to be fully appreciated.

Serves 6

3 tbsp extra virgin olive oil

1 small onion, finely chopped

1 small bulb of fennel, finely chopped

1 garlic clove, chopped

500 g (1 lb 2 oz) mixed fresh mushrooms, such as chanterelles (girolles), horns of plenty, oysters and chestnuts, roughly chopped

900 ml (1½ pints) boiling water

1½ vegetable stock cubes, crumbled, or 1 tbsp vegetable bouillon powder or paste

8 thin slices ciabatta bread

2 tbsp chopped parsley

2 tbsp chopped fresh mint

salt and pepper

Preparation time: 10 minutes

Cooking time: about 20 minutes

Each serving provides

kcal 95, **protein** 3 g, **fat** 5 g (of which saturated fat 1 g), **carbohydrate** 10 g (of which sugars 1 g), **fibre** 1 g

✓✓✓	B₁, copper
✓✓	B₆, C, niacin
✓	folate

1 Heat 2 tbsp of the oil in a large saucepan. Add the onion and fennel and cook over a high heat for 5 minutes, stirring frequently, until slightly softened. Stir in the garlic and mushrooms. Continue to cook, stirring frequently, for a further 5 minutes. Pour in the boiling water and stir in the stock cubes, powder or paste. Bring back to the boil, then reduce the heat and simmer the soup, uncovered, for 10 minutes.

2 Meanwhile, preheat the grill. Brush the slices of ciabatta bread lightly on both sides with the remaining 1 tbsp oil and toast them under the grill for about 1 minute on each side or until golden. Cut the bread into cubes and place in a bowl. Add the parsley and mint and toss well.

3 Taste the soup and add seasoning if necessary. Ladle the soup into bowls. Sprinkle with the parsley and mint croutons and serve at once.

Some more ideas

• For a rich and creamy version of this soup, thicken with a yolk and cream liaison. Whisk 1 egg yolk with 4 tbsp single cream until lightly mixed. When the soup is cooked and croutons prepared, remove the pan from the heat and stir a ladleful of the soup into the liaison. Pour the mixture into the pan and stir over a low heat for about 30 seconds. Do not allow the soup to get too hot and start to simmer or the egg yolk will curdle. Serve at once.

• Use 3 diced celery sticks instead of fennel.

• Dried wild mushrooms can be used for this soup, although it will take a bit longer to make. Use 1 packet of dried porcini, about 15 g, and 225 g (8 oz) chestnut mushrooms. Soak the porcini in some of the boiling water for 15 minutes and add them to the soup with the water. Cook the chestnut mushrooms in step 1 with the garlic.

Plus points

• In Asian cultures mushrooms are renowned for their ability to boost the immune system, and the Chinese have put them to medicinal use for over 6000 years. Mushrooms are a useful source of the B vitamins B₆, folate and niacin, as well as copper.

• Brushing slices of bread with oil and toasting under the grill before cutting them into cubes is a good way to make low-fat, crisp croutons.

Celeriac and spinach soup

Celeriac makes a rich soup with lots of flavour and a creamy texture. Young leaf spinach complements the celeriac beautifully, bringing colour and a light, fresh taste in the final minutes of cooking.

Serves 4

2 tbsp extra virgin olive oil

1 large onion, thinly sliced

1 garlic clove, crushed

1 celeriac, about 600 g (1 lb 5 oz), peeled and grated

1 litre (1¾ pints) boiling water

1 vegetable stock cube, crumbled, or 2 tsp vegetable bouillon powder or paste

500 g (1 lb 2 oz) young leaf spinach

grated nutmeg

salt and pepper

To garnish

4 tbsp single cream

fresh chives

Preparation time: 10 minutes

Cooking time: about 20 minutes

Each serving provides Ⓥ

kcal 150, **protein** 6 g, **fat** 10 g (of which saturated fat 3 g), **carbohydrate** 9 g (of which sugars 7 g), **fibre** 9 g

✓✓✓	A, folate
✓✓	C, B₆, calcium, iron
✓	E

1 Heat the oil in a large saucepan. Add the onion and garlic, and cook for about 5 minutes or until the onion is softened but not browned. Add the celeriac. Pour in the boiling water and stir in the stock cube, powder or paste. Bring to the boil over a high heat, then reduce the heat and cover the pan. Cook the soup gently for 10 minutes or until the celeriac is tender.

2 Add the spinach to the soup and stir well. Increase the heat and bring the soup to the boil, then remove the pan from the heat. Leave the soup to cool slightly before puréeing it, in batches, in a blender or food processor until smooth. Alternatively, you can purée it in the pan using a hand-held blender. The soup will be fairly thick.

3 Reheat the soup, if necessary, then stir in a little grated nutmeg, salt and pepper to taste. Ladle the soup into warm bowls. Swirl a spoonful of cream into each portion and garnish with fresh chives, then serve at once.

Some more ideas

● For a hearty winter soup substitute shredded spring greens for the spinach.

● Crispy bacon makes a delicious garnish for the soup. While the soup is cooking, grill 4 rinded lean back bacon rashers until crisp and golden. Drain on kitchen paper, then crumble or chop the rashers into small pieces.

● For a more substantial dish, add a poached egg to each bowl of soup.

● To make a delicious potato and watercress version of this soup, use peeled and diced potatoes instead of celeriac, and watercress instead of spinach. Add extra stock or semi-skimmed milk if the puréed soup is too thick.

● For a vegetarian main course soup, top with grilled tofu. While the soup is cooking, cook a 200 g (7 oz) block of tofu under the grill preheated to moderate. Allow about 3 minutes on each side or until browned. Cut the tofu into small dice and set aside. Toast 2 tbsp sesame seeds in a dry, heavy frying pan, stirring frequently, until golden. Ladle the soup into bowls, divide the tofu among the bowls and sprinkle with the sesame seeds.

Plus points

● Celeriac, a relative of celery, complements both the flavour and texture of spinach, making the most of the modest amount of cream used to enrich the soup. It also provides potassium.

● Onions have many health benefits. They contain sulphur compounds, which give onions their characteristic smell and make your eyes water. These compounds transport cholesterol away from the artery walls.

Kipper and sweetcorn chowder

With a few fresh ingredients, storecupboard standbys can be transformed into a great quick dish. Canned kippers and sweetcorn make a delicious chowder combined with leeks, potatoes and herbs. Serve with crusty rolls.

Serves 4

1 tbsp extra virgin olive oil

1 leek, thinly sliced

300 g (10½ oz) small new potatoes, quartered

600 ml (1 pint) boiling water

1 fish stock cube, crumbled

1 bay leaf

300 ml (10 fl oz) whole milk

1 can creamed sweetcorn, about 418 g

2 tbsp snipped fresh chives

2 tbsp chopped parsley

1 can kippers in oil, about 190 g, thoroughly drained and skinned

salt and pepper

Preparation time: 10 minutes
Cooking time: 20 minutes

Each serving provides
kcal 330, protein 15 g, fat 14 g (of which saturated fat 4 g), carbohydrate 40 g (of which sugars 7 g), fibre 4 g

✓✓	B$_6$, B$_{12}$
✓	C, folate, selenium

1 Heat the oil in a large saucepan. Add the leek and cook over a moderate heat for 2 minutes or until it is just softened. Stir in the potatoes and cook for a further 2 minutes. Stir in the boiling water, fish stock cube and bay leaf, and bring to the boil. Reduce the heat, cover and simmer for 15 minutes.

2 Remove and discard the bay leaf. Stir in the milk, creamed sweetcorn and half the chives and parsley. Use a fork to break the kippers into chunky pieces and add them to the soup. Taste the soup and add seasoning to taste, if necessary. Bring the soup to the boil, then immediately remove the pan from the heat to prevent the kippers from overcooking.

3 Ladle the soup into bowls and garnish each portion with a sprinkling of the remaining chives and parsley. Serve at once.

Some more ideas

● New potatoes stay in firm pieces in the chowder, but floury maincrop potatoes can be just as good, giving a slightly thicker texture as they break up slightly during cooking. Peel the potatoes and cut them into chunks.

● For a mackerel and sweetcorn chowder, use 200 g (7 oz) skinned, flaked and boned smoked mackerel fillets instead of the canned kippers. Pep up the chowder by stirring in 2 tbsp creamed horseradish with the sweetcorn.

● For a delicious crab and bacon chowder, rind and chop 100 g (3½ oz) smoked back bacon and fry with the leek in step 1. Instead of kippers, add 1 can crab meat in brine, about 170 g, with the liquor from the can.

● To make a punchy tuna chowder, add 2 crushed garlic cloves and the grated zest of 1 large lemon with the leek, and replace the kippers with 1 can tuna in spring water, about 180 g, drained. Add 1 seeded and finely chopped mild green chilli with the chives and parsley for the garnish.

Plus points

● Canned fish, such as kippers, pilchards and sardines, are an excellent source of calcium – the bones of small fish or fillets disintegrate in the canning process so they are eaten as well as the fish.

● Oily fish such as kippers (smoked herring) are full of omega-3 fatty acids, which help to lower blood cholesterol.

Quick chicken soup

This bright and easy recipe is perfect for a quick lunch or supper. Red pepper, sweetcorn and a sprinkling of fresh greens bring colour and texture to a simple chicken soup base, and adding a little sherry makes it taste just that bit more special. With seeded bread rolls it makes a tasty light meal.

Serves 4

900 ml (1½ pints) boiling water

2 chicken stock cubes, crumbled

1 red pepper, seeded and cut into fine strips

125 g (4½ oz) frozen sweetcorn

225 g (8 oz) skinless boneless chicken breasts (fillets), cut into short 1 cm (½ in) strips

125 g (4½ oz) purple sprouting broccoli, cut into small pieces, or spring greens, finely shredded

2 tbsp medium sherry

3 tbsp snipped fresh chives

3 tbsp chopped fresh tarragon

salt and pepper

Preparation time: 10 minutes
Cooking time: about 15 minutes

Each serving provides

kcal 140, protein 16 g, fat 4 g (of which saturated fat 1 g), carbohydrate 10 g (of which sugars 5 g), fibre 2 g

✓✓	A, C
✓	B₆, niacin

1 Pour the water into a large saucepan. Add the stock cubes and whisk over a high heat until the stock boils. Add the red pepper strips and sweetcorn. Bring back to the boil, then add the chicken strips and immediately reduce the heat to low. Cover and simmer gently for 5 minutes.

2 Uncover the pan and bring the soup back to the boil. Sprinkle the sprouting broccoli or spring greens into the soup, but do not stir them in. Leave the broccoli or greens to cook on the surface of the soup, uncovered, for 3–4 minutes or until just tender.

3 Take the pan off the heat. Stir in the sherry, chives, tarragon and seasoning to taste. Serve at once.

Some more ideas

• A generous amount of fresh tarragon gives this soup a powerful flavour. For a delicate result reduce the quantity of tarragon to 1 tbsp or use chervil instead.

• Use Savoy cabbage or curly kale instead of the greens. Trim off any very thick stalks before shredding the cabbage or kale.

• To give the soup a Chinese flavour, marinate the chicken strips in a mixture of 2 tbsp soy sauce, 2 tbsp rice wine or dry sherry and 2 tsp grated fresh root ginger for 10 minutes while you prepare the vegetables. Use pak choy instead of purple sprouting broccoli or spring greens. Slice the thick white stalks lengthways and the green tops across into ribbon strips. Add the white strips in step 2 and cook for 1 minute before adding the green tops. Add 2 chopped spring onions with the shredded pak choy tops. Cook for 2–3 minutes.

• Fine strips of lean boneless pork can be used instead of chicken.

• Add 75 g (2½ oz) dried thin egg noodles to make the soup more substantial. Crush the noodles and stir them into the soup in step 2 and bring to the boil before adding the greens.

Plus points

• Sweetcorn adds carbohydrate and dietary fibre to the soup. Green vegetables are also a good source of fibre, which is thought to reduce the risk of cancer of the colon.

• In this fast recipe, cutting fresh broccoli in small pieces and greens in fine strips means they cook quickly to retain as much of their vitamin C as possible.

• Red pepper is an excellent source of vitamin C, as well as beta-carotene and bioflavonoids.

Chilled leek and avocado soup

Coriander and lime juice accentuate the delicate avocado flavour in this refreshing soup. It is simple yet interesting, and ideal for a summer's dinner-party first course or a light lunch. Do not add the avocado too soon – not only will it discolour slightly, but its flavour will mellow and lose the vital freshness.

Serves 4

1 tbsp extra virgin olive oil

450 g (1 lb) leeks, halved lengthways and
   thinly sliced

1 garlic clove, finely chopped

750 ml (1¼ pints) vegetable or chicken stock,
   bought chilled or made with a stock cube
   or bouillon powder

1 large ripe avocado

125 g (4½ oz) plain low-fat yogurt

1 tbsp lime juice

2 tbsp chopped fresh coriander

salt and pepper

To garnish

8–12 ice cubes (optional)

slices of lime

sprigs of fresh coriander

Preparation and cooking time: 30 minutes,
   plus cooling and chilling

Each serving provides Ⓥ

kcal 170, **protein** 5 g, **fat** 14 g (of which
saturated fat 3 g), **carbohydrate** 7 g (of
which sugars 5 g), **fibre** 4 g

✓✓	B_6, C, E, potassium
✓	A, B_1, folate

1 Heat the oil in a saucepan, add the leeks and garlic, and cook for 10 minutes, stirring frequently, until the leeks are slightly softened but not coloured. Pour in the stock and bring to the boil. Cover the pan, reduce the heat and simmer for 10 minutes or until the leeks are cooked.

2 Remove the soup from the heat and let it cool slightly, then purée it in a blender or food processor. Alternatively the soup can be puréed in the saucepan with a hand-held blender. Pour the soup into a bowl and leave it to cool, then chill well.

3 Just before serving the soup, prepare the avocado. Halve the avocado and discard the stone. Scoop the flesh from the peel and press through a fine stainless steel or nylon sieve. The avocado can also be puréed in a blender or food processor until smooth, adding a little of the chilled soup to thin the purée and ensure it is completely smooth.

4 Stir the avocado purée into the soup together with the yogurt, lime juice and coriander. Add seasoning to taste, then ladle the soup into 4 bowls. Float 2–3 ice cubes in each bowl, if you wish, then add slices of lime and sprigs of coriander. Serve at once.

Plus points

● Half an avocado provides a quarter of the recommended daily intake of vitamin B_6 and useful amounts of vitamin E and potassium. Other substances in avocados are good for the skin.

● Leeks provide useful amounts of folate, which is important for proper blood cell formation and development of the nervous system in an unborn baby.

Some more ideas

● This soup is also good hot. Purée the hot soup with the avocado and stir in crème fraîche instead of yogurt.

● For a soup with Mexican flavours, cook 1–2 seeded and finely chopped fresh green chillies with the leeks.

● For a simple no-cook avocado soup, blend 2 avocados with 450 ml (15 fl oz) vegetable stock, then add the yogurt and lime juice, and season to taste.

● To make vichyssoise, the classic chilled leek and potato soup, increase the stock to 1 litre (1¾ pints) and cook 2 peeled and sliced potatoes with the leeks. Omit the avocado, lime juice and coriander, and serve sprinkled with snipped fresh chives.

Malay-style braised fish

Gentle braising is an excellent cooking method for fish, keeping it moist and succulent. Spiced with care and simmered in a little coconut milk, the fish here is delicious with plain noodles or rice. For a casserole with a livelier flavour, leave the seeds in the chilli or use one of the tiny, very hot Thai chillies.

Serves 4

1 tbsp sunflower oil

4 spring onions, chopped

1 red chilli, seeded and thinly sliced

2 celery sticks, thinly sliced

1 red pepper, seeded and thinly sliced

1 garlic clove, crushed

½ tsp fennel seeds

2 tsp ground coriander

½ tsp ground cumin

¼ tsp turmeric

1 can chopped tomatoes, about 230 g

120 ml (4 fl oz) coconut milk

300 ml (10 fl oz) fish stock, bought chilled or made with a stock cube

2 tbsp fish sauce or light soy sauce

1 can sliced bamboo shoots, about 220 g, drained

675 g (1½ lb) thick skinless white fish fillet, such as cod, hake, haddock or hoki, cut into chunks

16 raw tiger prawns, peeled

juice of ½ lime

To garnish

2 spring onions, chopped

1 tbsp chopped fresh coriander

Preparation time: 10 minutes

Cooking time: about 20 minutes

1 Heat the oil in a large frying pan. Add the spring onions, chilli, celery and red pepper, and fry, stirring constantly, for 5 minutes or until the vegetables are slightly softened.

2 Stir in the garlic, fennel seeds, coriander, cumin and turmeric and cook for 1 minute. Add the tomatoes with their juice, the coconut milk, stock and fish sauce or soy sauce. Bring to the boil, then reduce the heat and cover the pan. Simmer for 5 minutes.

3 Stir in the bamboo shoots, white fish and prawns. Cover the pan again and simmer for 5–7 minutes or until the pieces of fish are just cooked and the prawns have turned pink. Stir in the lime juice.

4 Serve the braised fish at once, garnished with a sprinkle of chopped spring onions and fresh coriander.

Some more ideas

• For a special meal, monkfish fillet can be used instead of the fish suggested in the main recipe. It takes slightly longer to cook, so increase the time in step 3 to 12–14 minutes.

• Chicken can be used instead of fish. Heat the oil and brown 4 halved, skinless boneless chicken breasts (fillets) for about 4 minutes on each side. Remove from the pan. Add the vegetables and soften as in step 1, then add 150 g (5½ oz) sliced mushrooms and cook for about 2 minutes. Return the chicken to the pan with the garlic and spices. Finish cooking as in the main recipe, using chicken stock and soy sauce instead of fish stock and sauce, and replacing the bamboo shoots with 1 can sliced water chestnuts, about 220 g, drained.

• Basmati rice with onion goes well with this dish. Soften 1 small onion in 15 g (½ oz) butter. Stir in 115 g (4 oz) basmati rice, then pour in 300 ml (10 fl oz) boiling water. Cover and cook over a low heat for about 10 minutes.

• Stir-fried noodles are also delicious as an accompaniment. Soak 250 g (8½ oz) dried medium Chinese egg noodles in boiling water for 5 minutes, stirring occasionally with a fork to separate the noodles. Drain the noodles well. Heat 2 tsp toasted sesame oil in a wok or large frying pan and add the noodles. Toss well for 1 minute, then stir in 3 tbsp light soy sauce and a little chopped fresh coriander.

Each serving provides

kcal 330, **protein** 47 g, **fat** 10 g (of which saturated fat 5 g), **carbohydrate** 7 g (of which sugars 6 g), **fibre** 2.5 g

✓✓✓	B$_{12}$, C
✓	iron, selenium, zinc

Plus points

● Fennel and fennel seeds are said to aid digestion and help relieve stomach cramps. In India toasted fennel seeds are chewed to prevent bad breath.

● Some studies have shown that chillies can help to reduce blood cholesterol levels. There are also reports suggesting that eating chillies can help to protect against gastric ulcers by causing the stomach lining to secrete a mucus which coats the stomach, thus protecting it from damage by irritants such as aspirin or alcohol.

Trout with green beans and pesto

This casserole is simple but stylish, relying on an unusual but complementary blend of ingredients rather than complicated techniques for a superb result. Serve with fluffy mashed potatoes or boiled new potatoes.

Serves 4

8 trout fillets, about 100 g (3½ oz) each

4 sprigs of fresh dill

250 g (8½ oz) green beans, halved

2 tbsp capers

200 ml (7 fl oz) dry white wine

300 ml (10 fl oz) hot fish stock, preferably home-made (see page 24)

4 tsp plain flour

2 tsp pesto

salt and pepper

sprigs of fresh dill to garnish

Preparation time: 10 minutes

Cooking time: about 15 minutes

Each serving provides

kcal 310, protein 41 g, fat 8 g (of which saturated fat 4.5 g), carbohydrate 6 g (of which sugars 2 g), fibre 1.5 g

✓✓	B$_{12}$, iron
✓	folate, selenium

1 Check the trout fillets for bones by running your fingers over the flesh. (Tweezers are useful for removing any stray bones, if necessary.) Lay the fillets skin side down and season them. Pull the fronds off the dill sprigs and sprinkle them over the fish. Roll up the fillets from tail to head end, with the skin on the outside, and set aside.

2 Put the beans in a large, fairly shallow pan – a frying pan or sauté pan with a lid is ideal, but a flameproof casserole can also be used. Arrange the fish rolls, joins down, on top of the beans. Sprinkle on the capers and pour in the wine and fish stock. Bring the liquid almost to the boil, then reduce the heat and cover the pan. Simmer for 12–15 minutes or until the fish and beans are just tender.

3 Mix the flour and pesto to a smooth paste. Use a draining spoon to transfer the fish rolls and beans to warm plates. Bring the cooking liquid to the boil. Whisk in half the pesto and flour paste until thoroughly combined with the sauce, then whisk in the remaining paste. Continue boiling, still whisking, for 2–3 minutes or until the sauce is lightly thickened.

4 Taste the sauce and adjust the seasoning if necessary, then spoon it over the fish and beans. Garnish with sprigs of dill and serve.

Plus points

• Trout is an oily fish, rich in omega-3 fatty acids, shown to help reduce the risk of heart attacks and stroke. They do so by thinning the blood, making it less likely to clot; lowering blood pressure and cholesterol levels; and encouraging the muscles lining the artery walls to relax, so improving blood flow to the heart. Omega-3 fatty acids also have an anti-inflammatory effect, which can help to relieve rheumatoid arthritis and the skin condition psoriasis. Other studies suggest that omega-3 fats may help to protect skin against damage from ultra-violet radiation and protect against skin cancer.

Some more ideas

• The casserole can be cooked in the oven at 200ºC (400ºF, gas mark 6) for about 20 minutes. Use an ovenproof dish or casserole instead of the pan suggested in step 2.

• Fennel tastes good with the beans. Halve and thinly slice 1 bulb, then place it in the casserole before adding the beans. Caperberries can be used instead of the capers – they are larger and look rather like small green olives. They have a strong peppery flavour, which is delicious with fennel and fish.

• Vary the herbs according to taste and whatever is plentiful. Try parsley, chervil, chives or tarragon, or a mixture of these.

• Beurre manié, made with 4 tsp plain flour and 20 g (¾ oz) butter (see page 18), can be used instead of the flour and pesto paste to thicken the sauce. Whisk in extra chopped fresh herbs for flavour before serving.

• For trout with leeks and thyme, flavour the fish rolls with fresh thyme leaves instead of dill. Heat the wine and stock in the casserole, then add 250 g (8½ oz) chopped leeks and 100 g (3½ oz) chopped celery. Place the trout on top, cover and simmer for 12–15 minutes. Remove the fish and vegetables. Thicken the sauce with beurre manié (see left) and add 2 skinned and chopped tomatoes, then pour the sauce over the fish.

Chicken jamboree

This healthy chicken and vegetable casserole makes an easy mid-week meal. To make it even quicker, you could use supermarket washed-and-cut carrots and broccoli, ready to go from packet to pan. Mixed wild and long-grain rice goes well with the casserole, and adds sustaining and nourishing carbohydrate.

Serves 4

2 tbsp extra virgin olive oil

350 g (12½ oz) skinless boneless chicken breasts (fillets), cut into small cubes

1 small onion, chopped

225 g (8 oz) button mushrooms

1 bay leaf

2 large sprigs of fresh thyme or ½ tsp dried thyme

3 large sprigs of fresh tarragon or ½ tsp dried tarragon (optional)

grated zest of 1 small lemon or ½ large lemon

150 ml (5 fl oz) dry sherry

300 ml (10 fl oz) boiling water

225 g (8 oz) baby carrots

225 g (8 oz) broccoli florets

1 tbsp cornflour

3 tbsp chopped parsley

salt and pepper

Preparation time: 10 minutes
Cooking time: about 20 minutes

Each serving provides

kcal 260, protein 23 g, fat 10 g (of which saturated fat 2 g), carbohydrate 11 g (of which sugars 6 g), fibre 4 g

✓✓	B_6, C
✓	folate, niacin, selenium

1 Heat the oil in a large sauté pan with a lid or fairly deep frying pan. Add the chicken and brown the pieces over a high heat for 3 minutes, stirring constantly. Reduce the heat to moderate. Stir in the onion, mushrooms, bay leaf, thyme, tarragon if used and lemon zest. Cook for 4 minutes or until the onion and mushrooms are beginning to soften.

2 Pour in the sherry and water. Add the carrots and seasoning to taste, and stir to mix all the ingredients. Bring to the boil, then reduce the heat and cover the pan. Simmer for 5 minutes.

3 Stir in the broccoli florets. Increase the heat to bring the liquid back to a steady simmer. Cover the pan and cook for 5 minutes or until the pieces of chicken are tender and the vegetables are just cooked. Remove and discard the bay leaf, and the sprigs of thyme and tarragon, if used.

4 Blend the cornflour to a smooth paste with 2 tbsp cold water. Stir the cornflour paste into the casserole and simmer for 2 minutes, stirring constantly, until thickened and smooth. Check the seasoning, then stir in the parsley and serve.

Plus points

• Broccoli and related cruciferous vegetables (such as cabbage and cauliflower) contain several potent phytochemicals that help to protect against cancer. Broccoli is also an excellent source of the antioxidants vitamins C and E and beta-carotene. It provides good amounts of the B vitamins B_6 and niacin, and useful amounts of folate.

• This recipe uses vegetables to extend a modest amount of chicken. Served with a starchy (complex) carbohydrate, such as rice, it makes a well-balanced meal, especially if followed by fresh fruit for a vitamin boost.

Some more ideas

● Semolina or fine oatmeal can be used to thicken the casserole instead of cornflour. Use 1 tbsp of either ingredient. Blend the oatmeal to a smooth paste with cold water and add as for the cornflour; sprinkle the semolina into the casserole, stirring, and continue stirring until the sauce boils and thickens.

● Small patty pan squash are good in this casserole. Trim off and discard the stalk ends from 225 g (8 oz) squash and slice them horizontally in half. Add them to the pan with the broccoli. When cooked, the patty pan should be tender but still slightly crunchy.

● For a creamy chicken and mushroom casserole, increase the quantity of button mushrooms to 340 g (12 oz) and leave out the broccoli. Simmer for 5 minutes longer in step 2. Stir in 4 tbsp single cream after thickening the casserole with the cornflour, then heat for a few more seconds.

● Ready-prepared stir-fry strips of turkey, pork or chicken are ideal for this casserole. They reduce preparation time and cook quickly.

Goulash in a hurry

This short-cut version of classic Hungarian goulash is rich and delicious. Strips of lean pork, shredded red cabbage and green pepper cook quickly and taste excellent with the traditional flavourings of paprika and caraway seeds. Serve rice or noodles and a simple green salad alongside, to complete the meal.

Serves 4

2 tbsp extra virgin olive oil
1 large onion, finely chopped
2 garlic cloves, crushed
3 thick lean pork loin steaks, about 300 g (10½ oz) total weight, cut into thin strips
1 tbsp plain flour
1 can tomatoes, about 800 g
120 ml (4 fl oz) extra dry white vermouth
2 tbsp paprika
1 tsp caraway seeds
1 tsp caster sugar
1 pork or chicken stock cube, crumbled
1 large green pepper, seeded and chopped
200 g (7 oz) red cabbage, finely shredded
salt and pepper

To serve
4 tbsp Greek-style yogurt
paprika
fresh chives

Preparation time: 10 minutes
Cooking time: about 20 minutes

Each serving provides
kcal 280, **protein** 21 g, **fat** 13 g (of which saturated fat 3.5 g), **carbohydrate** 16 g (of which sugars 12 g), **fibre** 4 g

✓✓✓	B$_{12}$, C
✓✓	B$_1$, B$_6$
✓	folate, niacin, iron, selenium, zinc

---

1 Heat the oil in a large frying pan or saucepan. Add the onion, garlic and pork, and cook over a high heat for about 3 minutes or until the meat has changed colour and become firm and the onion is slightly softened. Meanwhile, blend the flour with 4 tbsp juice from the canned tomatoes to make a smooth paste; set aside.

2 Add the vermouth, paprika, caraway seeds and sugar to the pan and stir, then add the tomatoes with the rest of their juice, breaking them up as you mix them in. Stir in the stock cube, and the flour and tomato juice mixture. Bring to the boil, stirring, and cook until the juices thicken.

3 Stir in the green pepper and red cabbage until both are thoroughly coated in the cooking juices. Reduce the heat, cover the pan and simmer the goulash for about 15 minutes or until the meat is cooked and the vegetables are just tender, but still slightly crisp.

4 Taste the goulash and season with salt and pepper, if necessary. Ladle the goulash into bowls and top each portion with a spoonful of Greek-style yogurt and a sprinkle of paprika. Garnish with chives and serve.

Some more ideas

● To make a vegetarian goulash, omit the pork and red cabbage. Cut 1 aubergine into large chunks and add to the softened onion and garlic in step 1 with 6 halved sun-dried tomatoes, 2 thickly sliced celery sticks and 2 thickly sliced courgettes. Follow the main recipe, using a vegetable stock cube or 2 tsp bouillon powder or paste. Simmer for 25 minutes or until the vegetables are tender, then stir in 1 can chickpeas, about 400 g, and 1 can red kidney beans, about 200 g, both well drained. Cook for a further 5 minutes. Serve topped with Greek-style yogurt or soured cream.

● Halved small new potatoes are good in the vegetarian version, above. Add them with the other vegetables and leave out the canned red kidney beans.

Plus points

● Several studies have shown that eating garlic can reduce the risk of heart attack and stroke by making the blood less sticky and likely to clot. Garlic can also help to reduce high blood pressure.

● Onions share garlic's healthy properties and they are also a natural decongestant. Using onions as the basis for everyday dishes contributes to good eating.

Bolognese beef pot

Lemon and fennel bring wonderfully fresh flavours to familiar braised minced beef in this Italian-inspired dish, making this as good for al fresco summer dining as for a light supper on a winter evening. Serve plenty of bread or rolls to mop up the deliciously tangy tomato sauce, plus a crisp leafy salad.

Serves 4

340 g (12 oz) extra lean minced beef

1 onion, chopped

2 garlic cloves, crushed

600 g (1 lb 5 oz) potatoes, scrubbed and finely diced

2 cans chopped tomatoes, about 400 g each

150 ml (5 fl oz) chicken stock, bought chilled or made from a cube

finely shredded zest and juice of 1 lemon

1 tbsp soft light brown sugar

1 bulb of fennel, thinly sliced

100 g (3½ oz) frozen green beans

salt and pepper

To garnish

chopped leaves reserved from the fennel bulb

chopped fresh flat-leaf parsley

Preparation time: 10 minutes

Cooking time: 20 minutes

Each serving provides

kcal 300, **protein** 26 g, **fat** 5 g (of which saturated fat 2 g), **carbohydrate** 40 g (of which sugars 14 g), **fibre** 5 g

✓✓✓	B₆, B₁₂, C
✓✓	folate, iron
✓	B₁, niacin, potassium, selenium

1 Place the minced beef, onion and garlic in a large saucepan and cook over a moderate heat for 5 minutes, stirring frequently, until the mince is broken up and evenly browned.

2 Stir in the potatoes, tomatoes with their juice, stock, half the lemon zest, the sugar and a little seasoning. Bring to the boil, then reduce the heat and cover the pan. Simmer the mince and vegetable mixture for 10 minutes, stirring once or twice to ensure that the potatoes cook evenly.

3 Stir in the fennel, frozen beans and lemon juice. Cover the pan again and simmer for a further 5 minutes or until the potatoes are tender and the fennel and beans are lightly cooked, but still crisp.

4 Taste and adjust the seasoning, if necessary, then spoon the mixture into serving bowls. Garnish with the remaining lemon zest, the chopped fennel leaves and flat-leaf parsley.

Some more ideas

• Use minced turkey, chicken, pork or lamb instead of beef.

• Carrots and canned beans can be used instead of potatoes. Add 1 can cannellini or black-eyed beans, about 400 g, drained and rinsed, and 250 g (8½ oz) finely diced carrots.

• If serving this dish to young children, do not add the lemon juice. Instead, serve with lemon wedges so the juice can be added to taste.

• A green salad tossed with thinly sliced red onion, a handful of fresh basil, a few black olives and a lemon and olive oil dressing tastes excellent with this dish, providing contrasting texture as well as flavour.

Plus points

• Extra lean minced beef contains 9.6 g fat per 100 g (3½ oz). Provided you use a heavy-based or good-quality non-stick pan, there is no need to add any fat when browning minced meat.

• Tomatoes are a rich source of vitamin C – fresh raw tomatoes contain 17 mg per 100 g (3½ oz) and canned tomatoes about 12 mg.

• Scrubbing potatoes rather than peeling them retains vitamins and minerals found just beneath the skin. The skin also provides valuable fibre.

• Frozen green beans are convenient and versatile for everyday dishes. They are a useful source of fibre and a good source of folate, which is essential for a healthy pregnancy. Folate may also contribute to protection against heart disease.

Moroccan-style pumpkin and butter beans

Middle Eastern spices flavour this low-fat vegetarian casserole, which is full of vegetables and other fibre-rich ingredients. It is a great recipe for a cook-ahead meal as the flavours mature and improve if the casserole is chilled overnight, then thoroughly reheated for serving. Try it with couscous.

Serves 4

600 ml (1 pint) boiling water

1 vegetable stock cube, crumbled, or
   2 tsp vegetable bouillon powder or paste

½ tsp turmeric

½ tsp ground coriander

pinch of ground cumin

200 g (7 oz) leeks, halved lengthways and
   sliced

225 g (8 oz) parsnips, cut into 1 cm (½ in)
   cubes

600 g (1 lb 5 oz) piece of pumpkin, peeled,
   seeded and cut into 1 cm (½ in) cubes

400 g (14 oz) yellow or green courgettes,
   sliced

1 red pepper, seeded and chopped

100 g (3½ oz) ready-to-eat dried apricots,
   chopped

1 can butter beans, about 400 g, drained

pinch of crushed dried chillies, or to taste
   (optional)

salt and pepper

To garnish

30 g (1 oz) pine nuts

chopped parsley or fresh coriander

Preparation time: about 10 minutes
Cooking time: about 20 minutes

1 Pour the boiling water into a flameproof casserole. Stir in the stock cube, powder or paste, the turmeric, ground coriander and cumin. Add the leeks and parsnips and bring to the boil. Reduce the heat to moderate, cover the pan and simmer the vegetables for 5 minutes.

2 Add the pumpkin, courgettes and red pepper to the pan, then bring the stock back to the boil. Stir in the apricots, butter beans and chilli flakes, if using, adding more to taste for a spicier result. Season with salt and pepper. Reduce the heat, cover the pan and simmer for 10 minutes or until all the vegetables are tender.

3 Meanwhile, toast the pine nuts in a non-stick frying pan over a moderate heat, stirring constantly, until just beginning to brown and giving off their nutty aroma. Tip the pine nuts onto a board and chop them coarsely.

4 Taste the casserole and adjust the seasoning, if necessary, then ladle it into deep bowls. Sprinkle with the chopped pine nuts and parsley or fresh coriander and serve.

Plus points

• Pumpkin is a rich source of beta-carotene and other carotenoid compounds. Save and roast or toast the seeds as a snack as they provide good amounts of protein and zinc.

• Dried apricots are an excellent source of beta-carotene and a useful source of calcium.

• Parsnips provide useful amounts of potassium, folate and vitamin B_1.

Each serving provides

kcal 250, **protein** 12 g, **fat** 7 g (of which saturated fat 1 g), **carbohydrate** 35 g (of which sugars 21 g), **fibre** 11 g

✓✓✓	A, C, iron
✓✓	B_1, B_6, folate
✓	calcium

Some more ideas

● This casserole is delicious ladled over couscous. Place 340 g (12 oz) couscous in a heatproof bowl. Add salt to taste and pour in 600 ml (1 pint) boiling water to cover. Cover the bowl and leave to stand for about 5 minutes or until all the water has been absorbed and the couscous is plumped up and tender. Add 15 g (½ oz) butter and fluff up the couscous with a fork to separate the grains.

● Try other vegetables with the pumpkin – for example, broccoli florets can be added with the pumpkin instead of the courgettes. The distinctive flavour of turnips is also good with the other vegetables.

● For a fresh, peppery flavour, garnish the casserole with 55 g (2 oz) grated red radishes or large white radish (mooli).

Family Favourites

Delicious, nutritious casseroles for every day

One-pot and cook-ahead meals are ideal for family cooking, which is what makes a casserole the perfect choice. Tempt your family with hearty Hungarian-style meatballs braised with potatoes and lots of mushrooms, or tender chunks of gammon simmered with sweet potatoes and juicy fresh pears. A cidered pork stew crowned with fluffy herb dumplings makes a super meal all on its own, as do savoury liver and bacon hotpot or a casserole of sausage chunks and macaroni with a crisp cheese topping. To make life very easy, put together a Creole-spiced bean pot and leave it to cook gently, then serve it with a vitamin-packed orange salad.

Hungarian-style meatballs

Minced turkey and mushrooms make succulent meatballs – delicious simmered in a sauce
of smooth passata with red and green peppers. Paprika warms the dish and new potatoes
turn it into a complete one-pot meal.

Serves 4

30 g (1 oz) butter

1 small onion, finely chopped

340 g (12 oz) mushrooms, finely chopped

340 g (12 oz) minced turkey

50 g (1¾ oz) fresh breadcrumbs

1 egg, beaten

2 tbsp chopped parsley

550 g (1¼ lb) small new potatoes

salt and pepper

4 tbsp plain low-fat yogurt to serve

fresh flat-leaf parsley to garnish

Paprika and pepper sauce

2 tbsp extra virgin olive oil

1 onion, finely chopped

2 garlic cloves, crushed

1 red pepper, seeded and thinly sliced

1 green pepper, seeded and thinly sliced

1 tbsp paprika

1 litre (1¾ pints) passata

pinch of caraway seeds

Preparation time: 35 minutes

Cooking time: about 45 minutes

Each serving provides

kcal 450, **protein** 27 g, **fat** 17 g (of which
saturated fat 6 g), **carbohydrate** 51 g (of
which sugars 19 g), **fibre** 7 g

✓✓✓	B₆, B₁₂, C
✓✓	A, B₁, B₂, folate, niacin, iron, phosphorus, potassium, zinc
✓	calcium, selenium

1 Melt the butter in a heavy-based frying pan. Add the onion and mushrooms, and cook over a moderate heat, stirring frequently, for about 10 minutes. The mushrooms give up their liquid initially, but this evaporates to leave the mixture greatly reduced, dark in colour and very thick. Transfer the mixture to a bowl and allow it to cool slightly.

2 Add the minced turkey to the mushroom mixture and use a fork to break up the mince. Add the breadcrumbs, egg, parsley and a little salt and pepper. Mix the ingredients until thoroughly combined. Wet your hands to prevent the mixture from sticking to them, then shape it into 20 walnut-sized balls. Set aside.

3 To prepare the sauce, heat the oil in a large flameproof casserole. Add the onion and cook for 4–5 minutes, stirring frequently, until softened but not browned. Add the garlic and red and green peppers, then continue to cook, stirring constantly, for 2–3 minutes. Stir in the paprika and cook for 1 minute, then pour in the passata and bring to the boil over a high heat.

4 Stir in the caraway seeds and salt and pepper to taste. Add the meatballs and the potatoes to the simmering sauce, taking care not to break up the meatballs. Bring the sauce back to simmering point, then cover and simmer gently for 35 minutes or until the potatoes are tender. Taste and adjust the seasoning, if necessary.

5 Ladle the meatballs, potatoes and sauce into bowls and swirl a little yogurt into each portion. Garnish with parsley and serve.

Some more ideas

● Omit the potatoes and serve the meatballs in their sauce with noodles or spaghetti.

● Replace the turkey with lean minced lamb and use chopped fresh thyme instead of the parsley. Add 2 cans flageolet beans, about 400 g each, drained, instead of the potatoes and several pinches of crushed dried chillies instead of the caraway seeds and paprika.

Plus points

● Minced turkey is a low-fat source of protein and a good source of zinc as well as vitamins B₁, B₂ and niacin.

● When eaten regularly and in quantity, potatoes are a useful source of vitamin C – new potatoes contain the most and eating them unpeeled retains the maximum goodness as the nutrients are concentrated under the skin.

family favourites

112

Spiced pork with sweet potatoes

This thoroughly modern casserole is a delicious example of fusion cooking, marrying ingredients and flavours from diverse cuisines. Oriental spices, sweet potatoes and fruit flavours go very well with the lean pork. Add bean sprouts and spring onions to a simple green salad to make a crisp, refreshing accompaniment.

Serves 4

1 tbsp sunflower oil

4 pork loin steaks or boneless pork chops, about 140 g (5 oz) each, trimmed of fat

1 red onion, coarsely chopped

2 celery sticks, chopped

1 large orange-fleshed sweet potato, about 400 g (14 oz), peeled and cut into sticks

150 ml (5 fl oz) sweetened cranberry juice

150 ml (5 fl oz) chicken stock, preferably home-made (see page 24)

1 piece of preserved stem ginger, drained and cut into fine sticks

1 tbsp thick-cut orange marmalade

1 tbsp dry sherry

1 tsp Chinese five-spice powder

2 star anise

4 plum tomatoes, quartered lengthways

salt and pepper

3 spring onions, shredded, to garnish

Preparation time: 30 minutes

Cooking time: about 30 minutes

Each serving provides

kcal 340, protein 34 g, fat 9 g (of which saturated fat 2 g), carbohydrate 32 g (of which sugars 16 g), fibre 4 g

✓✓✓	B_1, C
✓✓	A, B_6, B_{12}, E, iron, phosphorus, zinc
✓	B_2, folate, niacin, selenium

1 Heat the oil in a large flameproof casserole or deep sauté pan. Add the pork steaks and brown them for 3–4 minutes on each side. Transfer the pork to a plate and set aside.

2 Add the onion and celery to the oil remaining in the casserole and cook, stirring, over a moderate heat for 2–3 minutes. Add the sweet potato, cover the pan and sweat the vegetables for 3–4 minutes or until softened.

3 Stir in the cranberry juice drink, stock, ginger, marmalade, sherry, five-spice powder, star anise and a little salt and pepper. Bring to the boil, then reduce the heat and return the pork to the casserole. Cover and cook gently for 15 minutes.

4 Add the tomatoes to the casserole, cover and cook gently for a further 5 minutes or until the tomatoes are lightly cooked, but still hold their shape. Taste for seasoning, adding more salt and pepper if necessary, and serve, garnished with spring onions.

Some more ideas

● Add 400 g (14 oz) cubed pumpkin or butternut squash instead of the sweet potato, and 1 small bulb of fennel, chopped, instead of the celery sticks.

● Tomato rice goes well with this casserole. Bring 200 ml (7 fl oz) water to the boil and add 225 g (8 oz) rinsed basmati rice, 1 can chopped tomatoes, about 400 g, with the juice and 4 chopped sun-dried tomatoes. Cover and cook gently for 10 minutes or until the rice is tender and has absorbed all the water.

● For a rich fruit casserole, add 200 g (7 oz) pitted, ready-to-eat prunes and 2 cored and thickly sliced dessert apples instead of the tomatoes. Omit the sherry.

Plus points

● Sweet potatoes have a delicious natural sweetness that intensifies during storage and cooking. Although they contain slightly more calories than ordinary white potatoes – sweet potatoes have 87 kcal per 100 g (3½ oz), white potatoes 75 kcal – they are low in fat.

● Sweet potatoes are also an excellent source of beta-carotene and they provide good amounts of vitamins C and E.

● Lean pork has a lower fat content than beef or lamb. It is a good source of zinc and it provides useful amounts of iron.

family favourites

Cidered pork stew with light herb dumplings

A spoonful of mustard peps up this simple, vegetable-rich pork stew. Fluffy dumplings served on top help to mop up every bit of the full-flavoured sauce, and turn the stew into a well-balanced meal in a bowl.

Serves 4

1 tbsp extra virgin olive oil

450 g (1 lb) lean boneless pork, cut into 2.5 cm (1 in) chunks

2 carrots, cut into 1 cm (½ in) cubes

2 celery sticks, sliced

2 leeks, sliced

2 bay leaves

2 tbsp finely shredded fresh sage or 1 tsp dried sage

300 ml (10 fl oz) dry cider

300 ml (10 fl oz) pork or chicken stock, preferably home-made (see pages 24–25)

1 tbsp Dijon mustard

675 g (1½ lb) potatoes, peeled and cut into 1 cm (½ in) cubes

225 g (8 oz) swede, cut into 1 cm (½ in) cubes

salt and pepper

Fresh herb dumplings

100 g (3½ oz) fresh white breadcrumbs

55 g (2 oz) self-raising flour

½ tsp baking powder

3 tbsp snipped fresh chives

3 tbsp chopped parsley

1 egg, lightly beaten

3 tbsp semi-skimmed milk

1 tbsp sunflower oil

Preparation time: 30 minutes

Cooking time: about 1¾ hours

1 Heat the olive oil in a large flameproof casserole and add the chunks of pork. Cook over a high heat for 10 minutes or until well browned, stirring frequently. Use a draining spoon to transfer the meat to a plate.

2 Reduce the heat to moderate and add the carrots, celery, leeks, bay leaves and sage to the casserole. Cook for 5 minutes, stirring frequently, until the leeks are softened. Pour in the cider and stock. Return the pork to the casserole with any juices. Add the mustard and mix well.

3 Bring to the boil, then reduce the heat to low and cover the casserole. Simmer gently for 45 minutes, stirring occasionally. Stir in the potatoes and swede. Bring back to simmering point, cover again and cook over low heat for a further 30 minutes or until the pork and vegetables are cooked.

4 Meanwhile, prepare the dumplings. Mix together the breadcrumbs, flour, baking powder, chives, parsley and a generous pinch of salt in a bowl. Make a well in the centre of the dry ingredients and add the egg, milk and oil. Mix the liquids together, then gradually stir in the dry ingredients to make a dough.

5 Bring a saucepan of water to a steady but not too fierce boil. Dust your hands with flour, then divide the dumpling mixture into 12 portions and roll each one into a round dumpling. Keep dusting your hands with flour to prevent the mixture from sticking to them. Add the dumplings to the water, adjust the heat so that they simmer gently and cook for about 10 minutes or until risen and firm.

6 Taste the casserole and add salt and pepper, if necessary. Use a draining spoon to lift the dumplings out of the water, shaking gently to drain them well, and arrange them on top of the casserole. Serve at once.

Plus points

• Swede is a member of the cruciferous family of vegetables. It is rich in cancer-fighting phytochemicals and a useful source of vitamin C and beta-carotene.

• Leeks are thought to assist in preventing heart disease and stroke. They are also a source of vitamin E and their green tops provide beta-carotene.

Some more ideas

- If you are short of time, instead of making the fresh herb dumplings, serve the stew with pasta. Tagliatelle or penne tossed with chopped mixed fresh parsley and chives would be a delicious accompaniment.
- Serve herb scones with the stew instead of the dumplings. See Lamb and barley soup, page 74, for the recipe.

- To make a delicious savoury cobbler, preheat the oven to 180°C (350°F, gas mark 4). After bringing the stew to the boil in step 3, cover and transfer it to the oven to cook for 1 hour. Prepare herb scones (see page 74), arrange on top of the pork and vegetables and sprinkle with 40 g (1½ oz) grated Cheddar. Increase the oven temperature to 200°C (400°F, gas mark 6) and bake for about 15 minutes.

Each serving provides
kcal 510, **protein** 34 g, **fat** 16 g (of which saturated fat 4 g), **carbohydrate** 56 g (of which sugars 10 g), **fibre** 5 g

✓✓✓	A, B₁, B₆, B₁₂, C
✓✓	E, iron, phosphorus
✓	B₂, folate, niacin, calcium, selenium

Gammon with pears

Pears and sweet potatoes are delicious with gammon in this colourful casserole, and they make a relatively modest amount of meat seem more than enough. Serve with a mixture of lightly cooked broccoli and cauliflower and plenty of crusty French bread so you can enjoy every bit of the delectable sauce.

Serves 4

2 tbsp olive oil

340 g (12 oz) lean boneless gammon, cut into 2 cm (¾ in) cubes

2 onions, chopped

2 red peppers, seeded and diced

3 hard cooking pears

juice of 1 lemon

2 tsp soft light brown sugar

3 large sprigs of fresh thyme

600 ml (1 pint) vegetable stock, preferably home-made light (see page 23)

675 g (1½ lb) sweet potatoes, peeled and cut into 2 cm (¾ in) chunks

2 tbsp cornflour

a good pinch of freshly grated nutmeg

salt and pepper

sprigs of fresh thyme to garnish

Preparation time: 20 minutes

Cooking time: about 1 hour

Each serving provides

kcal 470, **protein** 29 g, **fat** 11 g (of which saturated fat 3 g), **carbohydrate** 67 g (of which sugars 32 g), **fibre** 8 g

✓✓✓	A, B$_6$, C, E
✓✓	B$_1$, B$_{12}$, copper, iron, phosphorus, potassium, zinc
✓	folate, niacin, calcium

1 Heat the oil in a large flameproof casserole. Add the gammon and cook over a fairly high heat for about 5 minutes, turning the pieces frequently until they are browned all over. Use a draining spoon to remove the gammon from the casserole and set the pieces aside on a plate.

2 Add the onions and peppers to the oil remaining in the pan. Stir well, then cover and cook for 10 minutes or until the vegetables are softened. Stir once or twice, scraping the bottom of the casserole to mix in all the browned cooking residue.

3 While the vegetables are cooking in the pan, peel the pears, quarter them lengthways and remove the cores. Toss the pears with the lemon juice so as to prevent them from turning brown.

4 Return the gammon cubes to the casserole. Add the pears with the lemon juice, the sugar and thyme, and pour in the stock. Bring to the boil, then reduce the heat to low and cover the casserole. Simmer gently for about 20 minutes or until the pears are tender.

5 Use a draining spoon to transfer the pears to a bowl; cover and set aside. Stir the sweet potatoes into the casserole and bring back to simmering point, then cover and cook for a further 10 minutes. Mix the cornflour to a smooth paste with 2 tbsp cold water and stir into the casserole. Bring to the boil, stirring. Reduce the heat, cover again and cook for 5 more minutes or until the gammon and sweet potatoes are tender.

6 Discard the thyme sprigs. Add the nutmeg and season with salt and pepper to taste. Ladle the casserole into shallow bowls and add the pears. Garnish with thyme sprigs and serve.

Plus points

● Pears contain vitamins C and E and a good quantity of potassium as well as natural sugars and soluble fibre (pectin).

● Gammon is a first-class source of protein, B vitamins (especially B$_{12}$), iron and zinc.

Some more ideas

• Gammon and pineapple are a popular combination and work well in this casserole. Add 8 slices of fresh pineapple or 1 can pineapple in juice, about 430 g, drained, with the sweet potatoes.

• Use ordinary potatoes instead of sweet potatoes. Cook for 15 minutes before adding the cornflour paste.

• Substitute 6 halved and stoned firm red plums for the pears, adding them with the sweet potatoes. Use oregano or marjoram instead of the thyme, adding fresh sprigs or ½ tsp of the dried herb.

• The casserole is also delicious made without sweet potatoes. Instead serve it with baked potatoes, couscous or rice or with mashed white potatoes.

Liver and bacon hotpot

This dish is dramatically different from old-fashioned liver casserole and a great choice for everyday healthy eating. It is bursting with flavour from the bacon, wholegrain mustard, peppery sage, carrots and swede. Serve it with some simply cooked green vegetables or a crunchy salad.

Serves 4

675 g (1½ lb) potatoes, peeled and thinly
    sliced

2 tbsp sunflower oil

400 g (14 oz) lamb's liver, sliced

2 back bacon rashers, rinded and finely
    chopped

2 onions, finely chopped

200 g (7 oz) swede, diced

200 g (7 oz) carrots, diced

2 tbsp plain flour

450 ml (15 fl oz) lamb or chicken stock,
    preferably home-made (see pages 24–25)

1 tbsp chopped fresh sage or ½ tsp dried
    sage

3 tsp wholegrain mustard

15 g (½ oz) butter

salt and pepper

Preparation time: 30 minutes
Cooking time: 45 minutes

Each serving provides

kcal 470, **protein** 29 g, **fat** 21 g (of which
saturated fat 6 g), **carbohydrate** 46 g (of
which sugars 9 g), **fibre** 5 g

✓✓✓	A, B_2, B_6, B_{12}, C, folate, copper, iron, phosphorus, zinc
✓✓	B_1, niacin
✓	potassium, selenium

1 Preheat the oven to 190°C (375°F, gas mark 5). Place the potatoes in a large saucepan and pour in enough boiling water to cover them. Bring back to the boil, then cook for 4–5 minutes or until they are just tender. Drain well but gently to ensure the slices do not break.

2 While the potatoes are cooking, heat the oil in a non-stick frying pan and brown the liver slices on both sides for about 1 minute, turning once. Transfer the liver to a casserole.

3 Add the bacon, onions, swede and carrots to the frying pan and cook, stirring, over a moderate heat for 10 minutes or until the bacon and onions are golden. Sprinkle the flour over the vegetables and stir it in, then stir in the stock. Add the sage, 2 tsp of the mustard and seasoning to taste. Bring to the boil, stirring.

4 Pour the bacon and vegetable mixture over the liver. Arrange the potato slices on top, overlapping them neatly and covering the vegetables and liver completely. Melt the butter in a small saucepan over a gentle heat and stir in the remaining 1 tsp of mustard. Brush the mustard butter over the potatoes and season lightly.

5 Cook in the oven for 45 minutes or until the potatoes are browned and tender. Serve straight from the pot.

Plus points

● Liver is an extremely rich source of iron and zinc, and of vitamin A and many of the B vitamins, especially B_{12}. The iron is in a form that is easily absorbed by the body.

● Swedes contain sulphurous compounds that are believed to help protect against cancer.

● Sage is a traditional herb for flavouring meats and liver, and it is thought to aid digestion, particularly of rich foods. It is also regarded as a calming herb and used to make a herbal tea that is thought to reduce anxiety and excessive sweating.

family favourites

Some more ideas

● For a Greek-style liver hotpot, use 200 g (7 oz) sliced button mushrooms instead of the swede and carrots. Stir in 2 tsp crushed coriander seeds with the flour, and the grated zest and juice of ½ lemon with the stock. Add 3 tbsp chopped parsley and 1 tbsp chopped fresh oregano in addition to the sage. Omit the mustard and sprinkle 1 tsp crushed coriander seeds over the potatoes after brushing them with melted butter.

● Instead of the potato topping, add dumplings to the liver and bacon stew. Cook the stew in a covered casserole for 25 minutes. Meanwhile, mix together 100 g (3½ oz) self-raising flour, a pinch of salt, 3 tbsp chopped parsley or mixed fresh herbs and 50 g (1¾ oz) shredded vegetable suet. Bind to a soft dough with 5 tbsp cold water. Shape into 8 balls, then add these dumplings to the stew. Cover and return to the oven to cook for a further 20 minutes.

Sausage and macaroni casserole

Here full-flavoured pork sausages, a generous portion of vegetables and tender macaroni simmer together in a red wine sauce, to make a delicious, hearty, healthy one-pot meal.

Serves 4

400 g (14 oz) high-meat-content pork
   sausages
2 tbsp extra virgin olive oil
1 tsp fennel seeds
2 bay leaves
2 garlic cloves, crushed
1 onion, chopped
1 tsp dried rosemary
1 tsp dried oregano
1 bulb of fennel, quartered lengthways and
   sliced across
1 aubergine, cubed
340 g (12 oz) small button mushrooms
4 tbsp tomato purée
300 ml (10 fl oz) red wine
600 ml (1 pint) chicken stock, preferably
   home-made (see page 24)
225 g (8 oz) macaroni
225 g (8 oz) red chard, finely shredded
85 g (3 oz) fresh breadcrumbs
3 tbsp chopped parsley
1 tbsp freshly grated Parmesan cheese
salt and pepper

Preparation time: 25 minutes
Cooking time: about 1¼ hours

1 Preheat the oven to 200°C (400°F, gas mark 6). Place the sausages in a flameproof casserole over a moderate heat and cook for about 8 minutes or until lightly browned. Turn the sausages frequently so that they brown evenly. Remove the sausages from the pan and set them aside on a plate. Discard excess fat from the pan.

2 Add the oil, fennel seeds and bay leaves to the pan. Heat until the oil is hot and the seeds are beginning to sizzle, then add the garlic, onion, rosemary and oregano. Cook, stirring, for about 5 minutes or until the onion is slightly softened. Stir in the fennel, aubergine and mushrooms.

3 Add the tomato purée, wine and stock. Stir to mix the tomato purée into the liquid, then bring to the boil. Remove from the heat. Slice the sausages and stir them into the casserole. Cover and cook in the oven for 20 minutes.

4 Stir in the macaroni and cover the casserole again, then return it to the oven. Cook for a further 15 minutes. The pasta will not be completely tender at this stage. Remove from the oven.

5 Reduce the oven temperature to 180°C (350°F, gas mark 4). Gradually stir the red chard into the casserole, adding more as the first handfuls wilt. Mix together the breadcrumbs, parsley and Parmesan cheese and sprinkle evenly over the top of the casserole. Put back into the oven, uncovered, and cook for 30 more minutes or until the topping is crisp and golden. Underneath, the pasta and vegetables should be tender. Serve at once, in the casserole.

Plus points

- Good-quality sausages with a high meat content are the best to use as they will contain less fat, fillers and additives. Read the label to be sure you are making a healthy choice.
- Red chard, a delicious leafy green vegetable, is a good source of beta-carotene, vitamin C and several of the B vitamins.
- Bay leaves are thought to act as a stimulant and aid digestion.

Each serving provides

kcal 750, **protein** 25 g, **fat** 37 g (of which saturated fat 12 g), **carbohydrate** 77 g (of which sugars 10 g), **fibre** 7 g

✓✓✓	C, copper, iron
✓✓	B_6, B_{12}, folate, calcium, phosphorus, zinc
✓	A, B_1, B_2, niacin, potassium

Some more ideas

• Try some of the more unusually flavoured sausages in this casserole. Pork and leek sausages and chicken and tarragon sausages are both good, as are Toulouse.

• Pork meatballs can be used instead of sausages. Mix 340 g (12 oz) lean minced pork with 3 crushed garlic cloves, 3 tbsp chopped parsley and 2 tbsp fresh breadcrumbs. Add 1 beaten egg and some seasoning and mix thoroughly. Wet your hands under cold water, then shape the mixture into walnut-sized meatballs. Brown the meatballs in step 1, then return to the casserole in step 3 in place of the sliced sausages.

Chinese-style lemon chicken

A savoury lemon sauce seasoned with a hint of sesame tastes fabulous with tender chicken and crunchy Oriental vegetables. Serve plain egg noodles or rice to add some satisfying starchy carbohydrate.

Serves 4

1 tbsp sunflower oil

425 g (15 oz) skinless, boneless chicken
  breasts (fillets), sliced

1 onion, halved and thinly sliced

1 large green pepper, seeded and cut into thin
  strips

1 garlic clove, chopped

1 tbsp finely chopped fresh root ginger

2 large carrots, thinly sliced at a slant

1 can water chestnuts, about 220 g, drained
  and sliced

300 ml (10 fl oz) chicken stock, preferably
  home-made (see page 24)

3 tbsp dry sherry

2 tbsp cornflour

2 tsp caster sugar

3 tbsp light soy sauce

1 tbsp toasted sesame oil

grated zest of 2 large lemons

juice of 1 lemon

150 g (5½ oz) fine green beans, cut into
  5 cm (2 in) lengths

225 g (8 oz) bean sprouts

Preparation time: 25 minutes

Cooking time: about 25 minutes

1 Heat the sunflower oil in a flameproof casserole. Add the chicken and cook for about 1 minute or until the meat is just turning white. Add the onion, pepper, garlic and ginger, and cook over a moderate heat, stirring often, for 5–6 minutes or until the onion is softened but not browned.

2 Add the carrots and water chestnuts. Pour in the stock and sherry, then heat until simmering, but not boiling rapidly. Cover and simmer for 10 minutes, stirring occasionally.

3 Meanwhile, mix the cornflour and sugar to a smooth paste with the soy sauce, sesame oil and lemon zest and juice. Stir the cornflour mixture into the casserole and bring to the boil, still stirring. Add the green beans, cover the casserole and simmer gently for 2 minutes. Stir in the bean sprouts and simmer for a final 2 minutes. Serve at once, before the bean sprouts soften.

Plus points

● Bean sprouts and other sprouted beans and seeds are rich in vitamins B and C.

● Canned water chestnuts are light and crunchy. Mixed with other vegetables, they can help to extend a modest amount of chicken or meat to make a satisfying meal. They also contribute small amounts of phosphorous and potassium.

Some more ideas

● Fresh shiitake mushrooms are good in this casserole – add 100 g (3½ oz) sliced shiitake with the green beans so that they will be just lightly cooked.

● Try 200 g (7 oz) baby corn instead of the water chestnuts and 200 g (7 oz) baby pak choy instead of the bean sprouts. A little chilli spice is good with this vegetable mix, so add 1 seeded and chopped fresh green chilli with the vegetables in step 1.

● This is a good recipe for firm meaty fish, such as swordfish. Cut the fish into chunks and add to the casserole in step 2, with the carrots and water chestnuts.

Each serving provides

kcal 320, **protein** 27 g, **fat** 12 g (of which saturated fat 2.5 g), **carbohydrate** 24 g (of which sugars 15 g), **fibre** 4 g

✓✓✓	C
✓✓	A, B₆, iron
✓	folate, niacin, selenium, zinc

family favourites

Stuffed turkey rolls with lentils

Tender turkey rolls filled with an apricot stuffing are delicious served on a bed of orange-scented Puy lentils, chestnuts and vegetables. The only accompaniment needed is a crisp leafy salad.

Serves 4

4 skinless turkey breast steaks, about 500 g (1 lb 2 oz) in total

1 tbsp extra virgin olive oil

1 onion, finely chopped

1 parsnip, cut into 1 cm (½ in) cubes

2 carrots, cut into 1 cm (½ in) cubes

1 tbsp plain flour

600 ml (1 pint) chicken stock, preferably home-made (see page 24)

2 tsp Dijon mustard

1 can whole peeled chestnuts, about 240 g, drained

200 g (7 oz) Puy lentils

2 tsp balsamic vinegar

salt and pepper

sprigs of fresh flat-leaf parsley to garnish

Apricot stuffing

1 onion, finely chopped

75 g (2½ oz) ready-to-eat dried apricots, finely chopped

2 garlic cloves, crushed

75 g (2½ oz) fresh breadcrumbs

3 tbsp chopped parsley

1 egg yolk

grated zest and juice of 1 orange

Preparation time: 40 minutes

Cooking time: 1¼ hours

1 Preheat the oven to 180°C (350°F, gas mark 4). One at a time, lay the turkey steaks between 2 pieces of cling film and bat out with a rolling pin into a rectangle measuring about 15 x 12 cm (6 x 5 in).

2 For the stuffing, put the onion, apricots, garlic, breadcrumbs, parsley, egg yolk, a third of the orange zest and 1 tbsp of the orange juice in a bowl (set the remaining orange zest and juice aside to add to the lentils later). Season the stuffing ingredients to taste and mix well together. Divide this stuffing among the turkey slices and use a fork to spread it over them, pressing it down evenly. Roll up each slice from a narrow edge and secure with wooden cocktail sticks in 2–3 places to keep the roll in shape during cooking.

3 Heat the oil in a flameproof casserole. Add the turkey rolls and fry over a moderate heat for 5 minutes, turning occasionally to brown them evenly. Use a draining spoon to transfer the rolls from the casserole to a plate.

4 Add the onion to the casserole and cook for about 5 minutes or until it is softened. Stir in the parsnip and carrots, then sprinkle in the flour and stir until it is evenly distributed. Pour in the stock and stir in the mustard. Add the chestnuts, and bring to the boil, stirring. Replace the turkey rolls in the casserole, cover and transfer to the oven to cook for 1¼ hours or until the turkey is tender.

5 About 30 minutes before the turkey rolls finish cooking, place the lentils in a large saucepan with plenty of cold water to cover. Bring to the boil and cook for about 20 minutes or until the lentils are tender. Drain the lentils and return them to the pan. Add the reserved orange zest and juice, and the vinegar.

6 Use a draining spoon to transfer the turkey rolls to a board and the vegetables to the pan of lentils. Lightly mix the vegetables into the lentils. Remove the cocktail sticks from the turkey rolls and slice them neatly.

7 Spoon the lentil mixture and some of the cooking liquid onto warm plates. Arrange the turkey slices on top. Garnish with parsley and serve.

Plus points

• Puy lentils are a good source of soluble fibre and a useful source of iron. Vitamin C in the orange juice helps the body to absorb the iron.

• Parsnips provide potassium and some of the B vitamins, including B_1 and folate.

Some more ideas

- Try ready-to-eat pitted prunes instead of apricots and use quartered baby turnips instead of parsnips. Reduce the stock to 450 ml (15 fl oz) and add 150 ml (5 fl oz) red wine. Omit the lentils and serve the turkey rolls and vegetables with mashed potato.
- For an Italian-style stuffing, use chopped sun-dried tomatoes instead of apricots, and 3 tbsp chopped fresh basil or 1 tsp pesto instead of parsley. Use a whole egg, beaten, rather than an egg yolk. After stuffing and shaping the turkey rolls, wrap 1 slice of pancetta or Parma ham around each before browning as in the main recipe. Omit the parsnips and carrots and instead add 1 seeded and finely chopped red pepper and 3 chopped celery sticks.

Each serving provides

kcal 600, **protein** 47 g, **fat** 11 g (of which saturated fat 2 g), **carbohydrate** 83 g (of which sugars 21 g), **fibre** 12 g

✓✓✓	B_6, B_{12}, copper, iron, phosphorus
✓✓	A, B_1, C, folate, niacin, potassium, zinc
✓	B_2, calcium

Squash and aubergine casserole

This colourful vegetable casserole is finished with a fresh and punchy mixture of parsley, garlic, lemon zest and toasted almonds, and served with fluffy Parmesan polenta. Touches like these can transform a simple vegetable dish into a feast for the eye and palate.

Serves 4

1 tbsp extra virgin olive oil

1 large onion, cut into 8 wedges

12 baby corn

1 small or ½ large butternut squash, about
    600 g (1 lb 5 oz), peeled, quartered
    lengthways, seeded and cut across into
    2.5 cm (1 in) slices

1 aubergine, halved lengthways and cut
    across into 2.5 cm (1 in) slices

1 Romano sweet red pepper, seeded and cut
    into 1 cm (½ in) pieces

100 ml (3½ fl oz) dry white wine

500 ml (17 fl oz) hot vegetable stock,
    preferably home-made light or rich (see
    page 23)

salt and pepper

Topping

2 tbsp slivered almonds

1 garlic clove, finely chopped

finely shredded or coarsely grated zest of
    1 lemon

5 tbsp chopped parsley

Parmesan polenta

200 g (7 oz) instant polenta

55 g (2 oz) freshly grated Parmesan cheese

2 tbsp chopped fresh oregano

Preparation time: about 20 minutes

Cooking time: about 45 minutes

1 Heat the oil in a flameproof casserole. Add the onion wedges and baby corn and fry over a moderate heat for 5 minutes, stirring occasionally. Preheat the oven to 180ºC (350ºF, gas mark 4).

2 Add the slices of butternut squash to the casserole, toss them in the oil and then stir in the aubergine and sweet red pepper. Cover and leave the vegetables to sweat over a low to moderate heat for 10 minutes, turning them twice, until they are lightly tinged golden brown. Pour in the wine, let it sizzle and then stir in the stock. Bring to the boil and add seasoning to taste. Cover the casserole and cook in the oven for 30 minutes.

3 Meanwhile, make the topping. Preheat the grill to high. Spread the slivered almonds on a baking tray and toast under the grill until they are lightly browned. Watch them closely and shake the tray occasionally to ensure the nuts are evenly toasted. Place in a small bowl and mix in the remaining topping ingredients.

4 To prepare the polenta, bring 1 litre (1¾ pints) water to the boil in a large saucepan over a high heat. Gradually whisk in the polenta and continue whisking until the polenta absorbs all the liquid. Reduce the heat

to moderate and cook for 5–10 minutes, stirring, until the polenta is thick. Beat in the Parmesan cheese and oregano with seasoning to taste.

5 To serve, spoon the polenta onto plates or into large individual bowls. Ladle the vegetable casserole on top and sprinkle with the topping.

Plus points

• Butternut squash is a good source of beta-carotene, which the body converts into vitamin A. Beta-carotene also works as an antioxidant, helping to prevent free-radical damage that may lead to certain types of cancer and heart disease.

• Sweetcorn provides fibre for keeping the digestive system in good shape.

• Parmesan cheese is a good source of protein and a rich source of calcium for strong bones and teeth. It also contains a high percentage of vitamin B_{12}.

Some more ideas

• Serve the casserole with potato and carrot mash instead of polenta. Cook 450 g (1 lb) potatoes with 250 g (8½ oz) sliced carrots in boiling water until tender, then drain well and mash with 5 tbsp semi-skimmed milk and 30 g (1 oz) butter. Stir in 55 g (2 oz) grated extra mature Cheddar cheese and 2–4 tbsp chopped parsley.

• Pearl barley is another delicious alternative to polenta. It can be cooked in the oven with the vegetable casserole. Put 170 g (6 oz) rinsed pearl barley in a casserole with 1 chopped onion and 1 tsp dried sage. Pour in 600 ml (1 pint) hot vegetable stock, cover and cook in the oven at 180ºC (350ºF, gas mark 4) for 45–50 minutes or until the stock is absorbed and the barley is tender.

Each serving provides Ⓥ
kcal 440, **protein** 17 g, **fat** 14 g (of which saturated fat 4 g), **carbohydrate** 58 g (of which sugars 14 g), **fibre** 8 g

✓✓✓ A, C

✓✓ B₆, folate, calcium, copper, iron, phosphorus, zinc

✓ B₁, B₁₂, E

Spiced lentil dhal

Potato and cauliflower are a favourite combination for curry and they are delicious cooked with lentils in a mildly spiced sauce. Served with a fresh carrot chutney and fruit and nut raita, this healthy meal will be relished by meat-eaters as well as vegetarians. Serve with basmati rice or naan bread.

Serves 4

2 tbsp sunflower oil
1 large onion, coarsely chopped
1–2 garlic cloves, crushed
2 tbsp finely chopped fresh root ginger
2 tbsp mild curry paste
170 g (6 oz) red lentils
1 tsp ground cumin
1 tsp turmeric
1 tsp salt
400 g (14 oz) small new potatoes, halved
1 small cauliflower, broken into florets
1 red pepper, seeded and coarsely chopped
4 tomatoes, skinned and quartered
225 g (8 oz) baby spinach leaves
generous handful of fresh coriander leaves,
   coarsely chopped

Carrot and coriander chutney

3 carrots, coarsely grated
1 green chilli, seeded and finely chopped
juice of 1 lime
2 tbsp chopped fresh coriander

Banana and almond raita

2 firm bananas
280 g (10 oz) plain low-fat yogurt
55 g (2 oz) flaked almonds, toasted

Preparation time: 25 minutes
Cooking time: about 55 minutes

1 Heat the oil in a large saucepan. Add the onion, garlic and ginger, and cook for 5 minutes. Stir in the curry paste and stir for a further 2 minutes over a gentle heat.

2 Stir in the lentils, cumin, turmeric, salt and 1 litre (1¾ pints) water. Bring to the boil, then cover the pan and simmer gently for 10 minutes. Stir in the potatoes and cook for 10 minutes, then add the cauliflower and cook for another 10 minutes. Add the pepper and tomatoes, and simmer for 5 minutes.

3 Meanwhile, prepare the side dishes. Mix together the carrots, chilli, lime juice and coriander for the chutney. Transfer to a serving dish. For the raita, slice the bananas into a serving bowl. Stir in the yogurt and sprinkle with the almonds.

4 Stir the spinach into the curry and cook for 2 minutes or until just wilted. Stir in the coriander and serve, with the chutney and raita.

Each serving provides   Ⓥ

kcal 550, **protein** 26 g, **fat** 17 g (of which saturated fat 3 g), **carbohydrate** 77 g (of which sugars 35 g), **fibre** 11 g

✓✓✓	A, B₆, C, E, folate, iron, phosphorus
✓✓	B₁, calcium, copper, potassium, zinc
✓	B₂

Some more ideas

• The vegetables can be varied according to whatever is available or preferred. For example, try chunks of courgette and aubergine with, or instead of, the cauliflower, or small whole okra or cut green beans with the tomatoes.

• Additional pulses can be added. Black-eyed beans and chickpeas are particularly good. If using dried pulses, soak them overnight, then drain and cook them in boiling water for 45–60 minutes or until almost tender before adding them to the curry. Canned pulses, well drained, should be added towards the end of the cooking time.

Plus points

• This curry is full of vegetables. Together with the lentils they provide valuable dietary fibre, vitamins and minerals.

• Vegetables play a protective role in fighting degenerative diseases and this recipe shows that eating 5 portions of fruit and vegetables daily can be easy and exciting.

• Uncooked accompaniments and salads boost the vitamin content of a meal as well as providing a variety of complementary textures and flavours.

Bean pot with orange salad

Creole spices enliven this hearty mixed bean and vegetable casserole. Like the classic French cassoulet, it has a crisp crumb topping. With the accompanying refreshing salad, it makes a tasty, well-balanced meal.

Serves 4

1 tbsp sunflower oil

1 onion, finely chopped

3 garlic cloves, crushed

1 tsp freshly grated nutmeg

1 cinnamon stick

2 bay leaves

1 can chopped tomatoes, about 400 g

1 tbsp tomato purée

2 celery sticks, thinly sliced

150 g (5½ oz) chestnut mushrooms, thickly sliced

1 tbsp dark muscovado sugar

750 ml (1¼ pints) vegetable stock, preferably home-made light or rich (see page 23)

150 g (5½ oz) dried flageolet beans, soaked overnight and drained

150 g (5½ oz) dried pinto beans, soaked overnight and drained

3 tbsp chopped parsley

150 g (5½ oz) fresh breadcrumbs

30 g (1 oz) butter, melted

salt and pepper

To serve

1 Cos lettuce

2 oranges

1 tbsp sunflower oil

3 tbsp flaked almonds, toasted

Preparation time: 20 minutes, plus overnight soaking

Cooking time: 3½ hours

1 Preheat the oven to 160°C (325°F, gas mark 3). Heat the oil in a large flameproof casserole and add the onion and garlic. Cook for 5 minutes over a low heat to soften the onion slightly. Add the nutmeg, cinnamon stick, bay leaves, tomatoes with their juice, tomato purée, celery, mushrooms, sugar and plenty of pepper. (Do not add salt now as it will harden the beans.) Pour in the stock and stir in the flageolet and pinto beans, then bring to the boil. Cover the casserole and cook in the oven for 2½ hours or until the beans are tender.

2 Discard the cinnamon stick and bay leaves. Stir in 2 tbsp of the chopped parsley and add salt to taste. Increase the oven temperature to 180°C (350°F, gas mark 4). In a bowl, toss the breadcrumbs with the melted butter until it is evenly distributed. Spoon the breadcrumbs over the beans and return the casserole to the oven, uncovered. Cook for a further 45 minutes or until the liquid has thickened and the breadcrumbs are golden.

3 Just before the bean pot has finished cooking, make the salad. Shred the lettuce and place in a salad bowl. Cut all the peel and pith from the oranges. Holding the oranges over the salad bowl, use a small sharp knife to cut the segments from between the membranes, allowing the juice and segments to drop into the bowl with the lettuce. Drizzle the oil over, add the almonds and toss together gently.

4 Remove the bean pot from the oven, scatter on the remaining 1 tbsp of chopped parsley and serve with the salad on the side.

Plus points

- Oranges are an excellent source of vitamin C, which helps the body to absorb the iron provided by the beans.
- Beans and pulses are rich in soluble fibre and have a low glycaemic index. This means they are broken down slowly so they are more satisfying, making you feel full for longer and keeping blood sugar levels stable.
- Almonds contribute protein to the salad accompaniment plus some vitamin E.

Each serving provides

kcal 550, **protein** 25 g, **fat** 16 g (of which saturated fat 5 g), **carbohydrate** 80 g (of which sugars 17 g), **fibre** 14 g

✓✓✓	C, E, copper, iron
✓✓	B₁, folate, calcium, phosphorus, potassium, zinc
✓	A, niacin

family favourites

Some more ideas

• Instead of almonds, add 2 coarsely grated carrots to the salad with 2 tbsp poppy seeds. Soak 2 tbsp currants in 2 tbsp orange juice for several hours or overnight, then add them with the carrots and poppy seeds.

• Peppery rocket is delicious with the oranges and almonds in the salad. Use 85 g (3 oz) instead of the lettuce.

• Instead of breadcrumbs, top the casserole with slices of garlic bread. Cream 1 crushed garlic clove with 40 g (1½ oz) butter and spread over 8 slices of French bread. Cook for only 30 minutes.

• Use all flageolet beans instead of a mixture of pinto and flageolet, or a combination of haricot and flageolet. Haricot with black-eyed or red-kidney beans is also good.

Special Casseroles

Healthy dishes for relaxed entertaining

Sharing good food with friends is fuss-free when the meal is based around a savoury casserole. Succulent beef in red wine with lots of baby vegetables is always popular, and pheasant braised with celery has fabulous classic flavours. Surprise your guests with more unusual casseroles: Indian-spiced lamb with yogurt and spinach, a rich ragout of duck legs or lean venison rolls with a cranberry stuffing. Finishing touches can make all the difference – chicken liver croutes perfectly complement a creamy blanquette of mushrooms, chestnuts and potatoes, and simply braised vegetables are made very special with little falafel and a cucumber and yogurt sauce.

Beef in red wine

Long, slow cooking gives this traditional casserole its inimitable flavour. The cooking liquid is reduced simply by removing the casserole lid, resulting in a wonderfully aromatic sauce that glazes the meat and vegetables. Flambéing with brandy brings the cooking to a spectacular finale. Serve with boiled or mashed potatoes.

Serves 4

2 tbsp sunflower oil

1 large onion, sliced

450 g (1 lb) lean stewing beef, cubed

250 g (8½ oz) baby carrots

250 g (8½ oz) baby parsnips

250 g (8½ oz) button mushrooms

1 garlic clove, finely chopped

1 bottle full-bodied red wine

grated zest and juice of 1 orange

1 sprig of fresh thyme

1 sprig of fresh rosemary

1 bay leaf

200 g (7 oz) shelled fresh broad beans, or frozen broad beans, thawed

salt and pepper

To finish

2 tbsp chopped parsley

3 tbsp brandy

Preparation time: 20 minutes

Cooking time: about 2½ hours

Each serving provides

kcal 390, **protein** 32 g, **fat** 13 g (of which saturated fat 4 g), **carbohydrate** 22 g (of which sugars 13 g), **fibre** 9 g

✓✓✓	A, copper, iron, zinc
✓✓	B₆, B₁₂, C, folate, phosphorus, potassium
✓	B₁, B₂, niacin, selenium

1 Preheat the oven to 150ºC (300ºF, gas mark 2). Heat the oil in a large flameproof casserole. Add the onion and cook over a moderately-high heat for 5 minutes or until softened and beginning to brown. Add the beef and fry for about 5 minutes, stirring frequently, until the pieces of meat are browned on all sides. Stir in the carrots, parsnips, mushrooms and garlic.

2 Pour in the wine, then stir in the orange zest and juice, thyme, rosemary, bay leaf, and some salt and pepper. Bring to the boil, then cover the casserole and transfer it to the oven. Cook for 1¼ hours.

3 Remove the lid and cook the casserole for a further 30 minutes, stirring once or twice. Stir in the broad beans and cook, uncovered, for another 30 minutes, again stirring once or twice.

4 Taste and adjust the seasoning, and stir in the parsley. Warm the brandy in a small saucepan and pour it over the casserole. Immediately set the brandy alight and carry the casserole to the table while still flaming.

Some more ideas

● Small broccoli florets or shelled peas can be added instead of the broad beans.

● For an everyday version, use 750 ml (1¼ pints) beef stock, preferably home-made (see page 25), or light ale instead of wine. Large carrots and parsnips, cut into equal-sized chunks, are more economical for an everyday stew than baby vegetables, and you do not have to flame the casserole with brandy.

Plus points

● Red meat such as beef offers excellent food value in a balanced diet – it is a good source of iron, zinc and vitamins B₆ and B₁₂.

● Robust broad beans go well with beef and they bring valuable dietary fibre to the dish.

Fragrant lamb with spinach

This enticing curry is warmly spiced rather than fiery hot with chillies. Serve it with basmati rice, chapattis and a fresh tomato and cucumber chutney for a healthy Indian-style meal.

Serves 4

2 tbsp sunflower oil

2 onions, finely chopped

4 garlic cloves, crushed

5 cm (2 in) piece fresh root ginger, peeled and chopped

1 red chilli, seeded and sliced

2 tsp paprika

2 tsp ground cumin

2 tsp ground coriander

1 tsp ground white pepper

½ tsp ground cinnamon

seeds from 8 green cardamom pods, crushed

2 bay leaves

½ tsp salt

200 g (7 oz) Greek-style yogurt

500 g (1 lb 2 oz) lean boneless lamb, cubed

2 large tomatoes, chopped

225 g (8 oz) fresh baby spinach

4 tbsp chopped fresh coriander

sprigs of fresh coriander to garnish

Preparation time: 20–25 minutes

Cooking time: 1 hour 20 minutes

Each serving provides

kcal 350, **protein** 32 g, **fat** 22 g (of which saturated fat 8 g), **carbohydrate** 7 g (of which sugars 6 g), **fibre** 2 g

✓✓✓	B$_{12}$
✓✓	A, B$_6$, C, folate, phosphorus, iron, zinc
✓	B$_1$, B$_2$, E, niacin, calcium, copper, potassium, selenium

1 Heat the oil in a large saucepan or flameproof casserole. Add the onions, garlic and ginger, and fry for about 15 minutes, stirring frequently, until the onions are golden.

2 Stir in the chilli, paprika, cumin, coriander, white pepper, cinnamon, crushed cardamom seeds, bay leaves and salt. Stir briefly over a moderate heat, then stir in the yogurt and 150 ml (5 fl oz) water. Add the lamb, mix well and cover the pan. Simmer gently for 1¼ hours or until the lamb is tender.

3 Add the tomatoes, spinach and chopped coriander. Cook for 2–3 minutes, stirring, until the tomatoes have softened slightly and the spinach has wilted. Taste for seasoning and remove the bay leaf. Serve garnished with fresh coriander.

Some more ideas

• The basic curry sauce in this recipe can be used to cook other meats or vegetables. Cubes of skinless boneless chicken or turkey breast (fillet) are delicious, as are lean boneless pork chops. All of these need only 40 minutes simmering in the sauce. A mixture of vegetables – halved new potatoes, cauliflower florets, sliced carrots and chunks of parsnip – is good too. Use 500 g (1 lb 2 oz) total weight and cook for 30 minutes.

• To make a refreshing fresh chutney to serve with the curry, finely chop and mix together 4 plum tomatoes, ½ cucumber, 1 small onion, 1 seeded fresh green chilli and 4 tbsp chopped fresh coriander.

Plus points

• Onions contain a type of dietary fibre called fructoligosaccarides (FOS), which is also found in chicory, leeks, garlic, Jerusalem artichokes, asparagus, barley and bananas. It is believed to stimulate the growth of friendly bacteria in the gut while inhibiting bad bacteria.

• Cardamom is believed to help relieve digestive problems such as indigestion, flatulence and stomach cramps, and it can help prevent acid regurgitation and belching.

special casseroles

Lamb-stuffed vine leaves

Stuffed vine leaves are popular in Middle Eastern and Mediterranean countries and there are many traditional recipes. This one is based on a classic Greek filling of lamb and rice but with added vegetables.

Serves 6 (makes about 40 parcels)

1 packet vacuum-packed vine leaves in brine, about 227 g, drained

1 tbsp extra virgin olive oil

1 bulb of fennel, chopped

1 red pepper, seeded and diced

1 green pepper, seeded and diced

2 cans chopped tomatoes, about 400 g each

2 garlic cloves, cut into thin slivers

150 ml (5 fl oz) vegetable stock, preferably home-made light or rich (see page 23)

juice of 1 lemon

salt and pepper

Lamb and rice filling

1 onion, finely chopped

170 g (6 oz) lean minced lamb

1 large courgette, diced

55 g (2 oz) pine nuts

170 g (6 oz) long-grain rice

2 tbsp chopped fresh mint

450 ml (15 fl oz) vegetable stock, preferably home-made light or rich (see page 23)

To garnish

lemon wedges

sprigs of fresh flat-leaf parsley

Preparation time: about 1 hour, plus 15 minutes standing

Cooking time: 1 hour

1 Rinse the vine leaves. Add them to a saucepan of boiling water and bring back to the boil. Blanch for 2–3 minutes, then drain the vine leaves and set aside.

2 For the filling, cook the onion and lamb in a non-stick frying pan for 5 minutes, stirring, until the lamb is browned and the onion is soft. Add the courgette and pine nuts and cook, stirring, for a further 3–4 minutes. Stir in the rice, mint and stock.

3 Bring to the boil, then reduce the heat and simmer, uncovered, for 7–8 minutes or until the stock is absorbed (the rice will not be completely cooked). Remove from the heat and season to taste, then set aside to cool slightly.

4 Preheat the oven to 190ºC (375ºF, gas mark 5). Snip off any long stalks on the vine leaves, then lay them out on a board with the veins uppermost and smooth sides underneath. (You will probably have to work in batches as there are about 40 vine leaves in a packet.) Place a heaped teaspoon of the filling in the centre of each leaf. Fold the sides of the leaf over the filling and roll up into a neat cigar-shaped parcel.

5 Heat the oil in a large flameproof casserole. Add the fennel and red and green peppers and cook, stirring occasionally, for 5 minutes. Stir in the tomatoes with their juice and a little seasoning. Add the vine leaf parcels to the casserole, pushing the slivers of garlic between them. Pour in the stock and sprinkle on the lemon juice.

6 Cover and cook in the oven for 1 hour or until the vine leaves are tender and the filling is firm and well cooked. Remove from the oven and leave to stand, covered, for 15 minutes. Garnish with lemon wedges and parsley sprigs before serving.

Plus points

• Pine nuts are a good source of vitamin E and potassium, and they also contribute useful amounts of magnesium, zinc and iron.

• Stuffed vine leaves are usually simmered in stock. Cooking them in a vegetable-rich sauce brings additional vitamins, beta-carotene and phytochemicals to the dish.

Each serving provides

kcal 300, protein 14 g, fat 11 g (of which saturated fat 2 g), carbohydrate 34 g (of which sugars 10 g), fibre 3 g

✓✓✓	C
✓✓	A, E, iron
✓	B$_6$, B$_{12}$, calcium, zinc

special casseroles

Some more ideas

• In the filling, bulghur wheat can be used instead of rice, and chopped almonds or walnuts instead of pine nuts. Add 55 g (2 oz) coarsely chopped raisins with the nuts.

• For a vegetarian version, omit the lamb and increase the amount of rice to 250 g (8½ oz). Cook the onion in 1 tbsp extra virgin olive oil until softened, then add 1 seeded and finely chopped red pepper with the courgette and pine nuts. Stir in the rice and stock and continue as in the main recipe.

• Serve warmed pitta bread with the casseroled vine leaf parcels, to scoop up the delicious sauce and vegetables.

Rich lamb and apricot couscous

Based on the Moroccan way of stewing meat with fruit, here lamb is marinated with mushrooms and aromatics, then cooked slowly with dried apricots. Shredded cabbage and fresh mint enliven the couscous accompaniment.

Serves 4

450 g (1 lb) lean boneless lamb, cut into chunks

340 g (12 oz) mushrooms, sliced

1 onion, thinly sliced

2 bay leaves

2 sprigs of fresh thyme

2 garlic cloves, crushed

2 carrots, sliced

2 celery sticks, sliced

¼ tsp freshly grated nutmeg

500 ml (17 fl oz) strong brown ale

1 can chopped tomatoes, about 400 g

150 ml (5 fl oz) lamb or chicken stock, preferably home-made (see pages 24–25)

150 g (5½ oz) ready-to-eat dried apricots, halved

salt and pepper

2 tbsp chopped parsley to garnish

Minted couscous with cabbage

750 ml (1¼ pints) boiling vegetable stock, preferably home-made light (see page 23)

450 g (1 lb) green cabbage, such as Savoy, finely shredded

340 g (12 oz) couscous

4 tbsp chopped fresh mint

Preparation time: 15 minutes, plus 12 hours marinating

Cooking time: 2½ hours

1 Place the lamb in a bowl with the mushrooms and onion. Tie the bay leaves and thyme together into a bouquet garni and add to the bowl with the garlic, carrots, celery and nutmeg. Pour on the ale and stir to mix, then cover and leave to marinate in the refrigerator for 12 hours.

2 Preheat the oven to 160°C (325°F, gas mark 3). Transfer the lamb, mushrooms and flavouring ingredients to a large casserole and pour the marinade over. Add the tomatoes with their juice and the stock. Cover and cook in the oven for 2 hours.

3 Discard the bouquet garni from the casserole. Stir in the apricots and return the casserole to the oven to cook for a further 30 minutes.

4 Just before the casserole is ready, prepare the couscous. Bring the stock to the boil in a large saucepan. Add the cabbage and bring back to the boil, then remove from the heat and immediately add the couscous and mint. Stir once, then cover the pan and leave, off the heat, for about 5 minutes or until the couscous has absorbed all the stock. Use a fork to fluff up the couscous.

5 Divide the couscous among 4 bowls and ladle the lamb casserole over the top. Scatter on the chopped parsley and serve at once.

Some more ideas

● Other dried fruits can be used instead of apricots. Dried peaches work well, as do cherries and pears.

● For a lower fat casserole, use joints of hare or rabbit or whole oven-ready pigeons instead of lamb. Venison is another good choice: use 450 g (1 lb) cubed stewing venison.

Plus points

● Surprisingly, dried apricots are a useful source of calcium. They are also an excellent source of beta-carotene and provide useful dietary fibre.

● Combining cabbage and mint with couscous brings flavour and beneficial nutrients along with the satisfying starchy carbohydrate.

Each serving provides

kcal 580, **protein** 37 g, **fat** 12 g (of which saturated fat 5 g), **carbohydrate** 76 g (of which sugars 31 g), **fibre** 8 g

✓✓✓	A, B₆, B₁₂, C, copper, iron, phosphorus
✓✓	B₁, B₂, folate, niacin, calcium, potassium, zinc
✓	selenium

✓✓✓	A, B_6, B_{12}, C, copper, iron, phosphorus
✓✓	B_1, B_2, folate, niacin, calcium, potassium, zinc
✓	selenium

special casseroles

Venison olives

Olive is the traditional term for a small roll of meat filled with stuffing. For this special-occasion casserole thin slices of tender lean venison are rolled round a fresh-tasting cranberry stuffing and cooked in a red wine sauce.

Serves 4

550 g (1¼ lb) boneless leg of venison, cut into 4 thin slices

2 tbsp sunflower oil

2 sprigs of fresh thyme

1 bay leaf

10 black peppercorns, lightly crushed

8 juniper berries, lightly crushed

4 cloves

120 ml (4 fl oz) beef stock, preferably home-made (see page 25)

360 ml (12 fl oz) red wine

55 g (2 oz) cranberries, thawed if frozen, finely chopped

1 carrot, thinly sliced

1 onion, sliced

1 garlic clove, sliced

salt and pepper

leaves of fresh thyme to garnish

Cranberry stuffing

30 g (1 oz) cranberries, thawed if frozen

45 g (1½ oz) fresh wholemeal breadcrumbs

finely grated zest of 1 orange

30 g (1 oz) carrot, finely grated

2 tsp fresh thyme leaves

2 tbsp orange juice

Preparation time: 20 minutes

Cooking time: about 1 hour

1 First make the stuffing. Mix the cranberries with the breadcrumbs, orange zest, carrot, thyme and orange juice until thoroughly combined.

2 Place each slice of venison in turn between 2 sheets of cling film and use a rolling pin to bat them out until they are thin. Lay a slice of venison on a board and place a quarter of the stuffing in the centre. Flatten the stuffing slightly, leaving a border all around it, then fold the sides of the meat over it. Roll up the meat to enclose the stuffing in a neat package. Secure with a wooden cocktail stick. Repeat with the remaining venison slices and stuffing.

3 Heat the oil in a flameproof casserole. Add the venison olives and cook for about 6 minutes, rolling them occasionally so that they brown evenly. Meanwhile, place the thyme, bay leaf, peppercorns, juniper berries and cloves in a small square of muslin or fine cotton fabric and tie up into a bouquet garni. Add to the casserole together with the stock, wine, cranberries, carrot, onion and garlic. Bring slowly to the boil, then reduce the heat to low, cover and simmer for 40 minutes or until the venison is very tender.

4 Discard the bouquet garni. Use a draining spoon to transfer the venison olives to a warm serving dish.

Cover and keep warm. Transfer the cooked vegetables to a blender and add a ladleful of the cooking liquid, then purée until smooth. Boil the remaining cooking liquid over high heat for 2–3 minutes or until reduced slightly. Return the puréed vegetables to the pan, stir and reheat.

5 Remove the cocktail sticks from the venison olives, then slice them and arrange on warmed plates with some of the sauce. Offer the remaining sauce separately. Garnish with fresh thyme sprigs and serve.

Plus points

- Cranberries are rich in vitamin C. They also contain a natural antibiotic that prevents the bacteria which cause cystitis from sticking to the walls of the bladder.
- Venison is a good choice for rich casseroles as it has a lot of flavour with very little fat compared to red meat or chicken.

Each serving provides

kcal 300, **protein** 33 g, **fat** 8 g (of which saturated fat 2 g), **carbohydrate** 16 g (of which sugars 3 g), **fibre** 2 g

✓✓	A, iron, phosphorus, potassium
✓	B₂, C, E, copper, zinc

Some more ideas

● Small venison steaks are also ideal for making olives. Alternatively, lean slices of beef topside can be used instead of the venison.

● Mushrooms make a delicious replacement for cranberries in the stuffing, especially if the olives are served with a garlic-flavoured sauce. Make the stuffing with 45 g (1½ oz) wholemeal breadcrumbs, 100 g (3½ oz) chopped brown cap mushrooms, 1 tbsp chopped shallot, 1 chopped garlic clove and 1 tbsp chopped parsley. Pound the ingredients with a spoon so that they bind together. Omit the bouquet garni and instead add the peeled cloves from 1 large head of garlic. By the time the venison olives are tender, the garlic will be soft and mellowed in flavour. Purée the garlic with the vegetables as in the main recipe.

One-pot Japanese chicken

Based on Japanese-style fondues, in which food is cooked at the table in a flavoursome broth, this chicken and vegetable casserole makes a satisfying main course all in one pot. A sharp and savoury citrus sauce provides a delicious dip to season the succulent ingredients individually just before they are eaten.

Serves 4

225 g (8 oz) fine rice noodles

600 ml (1 pint) chicken stock, preferably home-made (see page 24)

550 g (1¼ lb) skinless boneless chicken breasts (fillets), thinly sliced

225 g (8 oz) carrots, sliced

200 g (7 oz) mange-tout

1 can sliced bamboo shoots, about 220 g, drained

125 g (4½ oz) shiitake mushrooms, sliced

115 g (4 oz) Chinese leaves, shredded

Ponzu sauce

3 tbsp mirin (sweet rice wine)

juice of 1 lemon

juice of 1½ limes

3 tbsp rice vinegar

90 ml (3 fl oz) dark soy sauce

Preparation time: 15 minutes, plus 10 minutes soaking

Cooking time: about 30 minutes

Each serving provides

kcal 500, **protein** 38 g, **fat** 7 g (of which saturated fat 2 g), **carbohydrate** 60 g (of which sugars 7 g), **fibre** 4 g

✓✓	A, C, B₆, niacin, copper, iron
✓	B₁, B₂, folate, potassium, selenium, zinc

1 The ponzu sauce can be made a day or more in advance. Pour the mirin into a small saucepan, bring to the boil over a high heat and boil for 30 seconds so that the alcohol evaporates. Stir in all the remaining sauce ingredients and remove from the heat. Pour into a dish, cover and set aside.

2 Place the noodles in a bowl and pour in cold water to cover. Leave to soak for 10 minutes, then drain and set aside. Bring the chicken stock to the boil in a large flameproof casserole. Reduce the heat so that the stock simmers, then add the chicken pieces and simmer for 10 minutes.

3 Stir in the carrots and bring back to simmering point, then cook for 5 minutes. Add the mange-tout and bamboo shoots and simmer for a further 2–3 minutes. Stir in the mushrooms and shredded Chinese leaves, bring back to simmering point again and cook for 2–3 minutes. Finally, stir in the rice noodles, bring back to simmering point and cook for 2–3 minutes or until the noodles are hot.

4 Divide the ponzu sauce among 4 small bowls. Ladle the casserole into warm serving bowls. Serve at once, offering the ponzu sauce with the casserole, so that bite-sized pieces can be dipped before they are eaten.

Some more ideas

● Replace the Chinese leaves with the leaves from a bunch of watercress and 115 g (4 oz) young spinach leaves.

● Tofu works well in this dish to make a vegetarian casserole. Replace the chicken with 450 g (1 lb) firm tofu, cut into 3.5 cm (1½ in) cubes, adding it with the carrots, and use vegetable stock.

● For a Japanese seafood pot, use 450 g (1 lb) chunks of firm white fish, such as cod or sea bream, instead of the chicken and reduce the cooking time in step 2 to 5 minutes. Use fish stock, and add 12 large peeled raw prawns with the mushrooms.

● Instead of chicken, make this casserole with 450 g (1 lb) fillet steak and use beef stock. Simmer the steak for 5 minutes before adding the carrots.

Plus points

● Mange-tout are an excellent source of vitamin C and they also provide beta-carotene, potassium and fibre.

● Soy sauce is a popular condiment in Oriental cooking. It is a concentrated source of sodium, so it is diluted for this sauce with fresh citrus juice, rice wine and rice vinegar.

Duck ragout with mustard croutes

Duck legs become beautifully succulent when slow-cooked with wine and vegetables, and are very lean without the skin. Boiling the cooking liquid to reduce it results in a sauce with a wonderful flavour, which is great soaked up by the crisp, piquant bread croutes that accompany the dish.

Serves 4

1 tbsp extra virgin olive oil

4 duck leg joints, about 800–900 g
 (1¾–2 lb) in total, skinned

250 g (8½ oz) button mushrooms

250 g (8½ oz) pickling onions, shallots or
 button onions

2–4 garlic cloves, finely chopped

½ tsp dried thyme

1 bay leaf

300 ml (10 fl oz) red wine

750 ml (1¼ pints) chicken stock, preferably
 home-made (see page 24)

250 g (8½ oz) baby carrots

250 g (8½ oz) baby turnips, halved if large

250 g (8½ oz) sugarsnap peas

2 tsp redcurrant jelly

salt and pepper

sprigs of fresh mint to garnish

Mustard croutes

1 tbsp extra virgin olive oil

1 tbsp Dijon mustard

12 thick slices of French bread

Preparation time: 30 minutes

Cooking time: about 1½ hours

1 Heat the oil in a large flameproof casserole over a moderate heat. Add the duck and cook for about 10 minutes, turning the pieces so that they brown lightly on both sides. Use a draining spoon to transfer the duck to a plate.

2 Add the mushrooms, onions, garlic, thyme and bay leaf to the casserole. Increase the heat slightly and fry for 4 minutes, stirring frequently, until the vegetables begin to colour.

3 Pour in the wine and let it bubble briefly. Return the duck to the pan with any accumulated juices. Add the stock and bring to the boil. Reduce the heat to low, cover the casserole and simmer, stirring occasionally, for 30 minutes. Add the carrots and turnips, pushing them into the liquid. Cover and continue simmering for 15 minutes. Add the sugarsnap peas and cook for a further 5–10 minutes or until the duck and vegetables are tender

4 Meanwhile, make the croutes. Preheat the oven to 190ºC (375ºF, gas mark 5). Mix the oil with the mustard and spread thinly over the slices of bread. Place on a baking tray and bake for 10–12 minutes or until crisp and browned.

5 If necessary, use a metal spoon to skim off any fat from the surface of the liquid in the casserole. Place a

colander or strainer over a large saucepan. Drain the duck and vegetables, then return them to the casserole, discarding the bay leaf. Cover the casserole and set it aside. Boil the strained cooking liquid vigorously over a high heat for about 10–12 minutes or until reduced by about half to a rich, full-flavoured sauce. Stir in the redcurrant jelly until it has melted, then add seasoning to taste.

6 Arrange the croutes on the duck and vegetables – any that do not fit in the casserole can be served separately. Spoon the sauce over the top, allowing some to soak into the croutes. Garnish with mint sprigs and serve.

Plus points

• Duck is a good source of many of the B vitamins, iron and zinc. Weight for weight, it contains over twice as much B_1 and B_2 as chicken, and three times as much iron.

• Red wine is rich in flavonoids, which can help to protect against heart disease and stroke. Cabernet Sauvignon, Merlot and Pinot Noir wines, particularly from Chile, have higher levels of flavonoids than other wines.

special casseroles

Some more ideas

● Guinea fowl or pheasant portions are also delicious cooked this way, as are chicken leg quarters. For chicken you could use white wine for a lighter sauce.

● Another alternative is venison, which goes very well with the robust flavours in the red wine sauce. Use 4 small tender venison steaks, about 800–900 g (1¾–2 lb) in total, and brown them briefly on both sides in step 1.

● Vary the vegetables according to what is available. Scrubbed Fir Apple potatoes are a delicious addition and baby parsnips can be used instead of the turnips. Try French beans or baby courgettes instead of the sugarsnap peas or substitute button Brussels sprouts.

Each serving provides

kcal 650, **protein** 46 g, **fat** 16 g (of which saturated fat 3 g), **carbohydrate** 73 g (of which sugars 17 g), **fibre** 7.5 g

✓✓✓ B₆, B₁₂, C, copper, iron, phosphorus

✓✓ A, B₁, B₂, folate, niacin, calcium

✓ potassium, selenium, zinc

Pheasant and celery casserole

Juniper berries and orange flavour the sauce, while walnuts contribute a satisfying crunch to this excellent winter casserole. It is served with a warming mash of carrots, parsnips and potatoes – perfect with the pheasant.

Serves 4

2 tbsp extra virgin olive oil

4 boneless pheasant breast fillets, about 400 g (14 oz) in total

1 onion, finely chopped

3 dessert apples, such as Cox's

2 celery hearts, halved lengthways

strip of pared orange zest

juice of 1 orange

1 tsp juniper berries, lightly crushed

400 ml (14 fl oz) game or chicken stock, preferably home-made (see page 24)

85 g (3 oz) walnut halves

salt and pepper

Golden mash

4 carrots, cut into chunks

450 g (1 lb) potatoes, peeled and cut into chunks

2 large parsnip, cut into chunks

100 ml (3½ fl oz) semi-skimmed milk

Preparation time: 30 minutes

Cooking time: 40–45 minutes

Each serving provides

kcal 650, **protein** 42 g, **fat** 32 g (of which saturated fat 6 g), **carbohydrate** 52 g (of which sugars 26 g), **fibre** 10 g

✓✓✓	B₆, B₁₂, C, iron, phosphorus
✓✓	A, folate, copper, potassium, zinc
✓	B₁, B₂, niacin, calcium, selenium

1 Preheat the oven to 180°C (350°F, gas mark 4). Heat the oil in a flameproof casserole. Add the pheasant fillets and cook over a high heat for 1–2 minutes, turning to brown both sides. Use a draining spoon to remove them from the pan and set aside.

2 Add the onion to the casserole, reduce the heat to low and cook gently for about 5 minutes or until softened but not browned. Peel, core and dice 2 of the apples and add to the casserole (reserve the third apple for garnishing). If the celery is too long to fit in the casserole, cut it across in half, then add to the casserole with the orange zest and juice, juniper berries, stock and walnuts. Season lightly and bring to the boil over a moderate heat.

3 Return the pheasant fillets to the casserole, tucking them under the celery. Cover tightly and transfer to the oven to cook for 20–25 minutes or until the pheasant is tender. The celery should still be quite firm. Do not overcook or the pheasant will become dry and the celery too soft.

4 Meanwhile, prepare the mash. Put the vegetables in a large saucepan and pour in just enough boiling water to cover. Add salt to taste and bring back to the boil. Reduce the heat, cover the pan and simmer for about 20 minutes or until the vegetables are tender.

5 Tip the cooked vegetables into a colander to drain. Pour the milk into the pan and place over a high heat. When the milk is hot, remove from the heat and return the vegetables to the pan. Mash the vegetables with the milk and seasoning to taste until smooth. Cover the pan to keep the mash hot while you finish the casserole.

6 Use a draining spoon to transfer the pheasant, celery, apples and walnuts to a warm dish. Cover and keep hot. Discard the orange zest, then bring the cooking liquid to the boil over a high heat. Boil hard for about 5 minutes or until the liquid is reduced and slightly syrupy in consistency.

7 Meanwhile, quarter and core the apple for the garnish, then cut it into neat slices. Divide the mash among 4 plates and top with the celery, apples and walnuts. Slice the pheasant and arrange on the celery. Taste the sauce for seasoning, then spoon it over the pheasant and celery. Garnish with the apple slices and serve.

Plus points

- Pheasant is low in fat and an excellent source of iron and B vitamins.
- Celery contains a compound called phthalide that is believed to help lower high blood pressure.

Some more ideas

- Replace the pheasant fillets with 1 jointed pheasant and increase the cooking time in step 3 to 40–45 minutes. Add the celery halfway through the time to avoid overcooking it.
- Root vegetables are delicious in the casserole with the pheasant. Omit the onion, celery, apples and walnuts. Instead, in step 2 brown 100 g (3½ oz) shallots, then push them to one side of the pan. Add 200 g (7 oz) baby leeks and toss over a high heat for 2 minutes, then add 200 g (7 oz) each of baby carrots and parsnips. Replace the pheasant and finish as in the main recipe.
- Use skinless boneless chicken breasts (fillets) or turkey breast fillets instead of pheasant.
- Fennel is a delicious alternative to the celery – use 4 bulbs cut lengthways in half.

Blanquette with pâté croutes

The classic blanquette is a stew of poultry, veal or pork in a rich white sauce. In this contemporary version tender vegetables and chestnuts in a creamy sauce are partnered by savoury chicken liver croutes.

Serves 4

1 tbsp extra virgin olive oil

2 leeks, white parts only, thickly sliced

12 button onions or pickling onions, peeled

2 bay leaves

2 tbsp plain flour

450 ml (15 fl oz) chicken stock, preferably home-made (see page 24)

150 ml (5 fl oz) dry white wine

450 g (1 lb) new potatoes

450 g (1 lb) small button mushrooms

1 can peeled chestnuts, about 240 g, drained

1 egg yolk

2 tbsp single cream

pinch of freshly grated nutmeg

salt and pepper

fresh tarragon to garnish

Pâté croutes

2 tbsp extra virgin olive oil

1 short French loaf, cut into 12 slices

1 shallot, finely chopped

1 garlic clove, finely chopped

2 lean back bacon rashers, rinded and finely chopped

200 g (7 oz) chicken livers, coarsely chopped

2 tsp chopped fresh tarragon

4 tbsp chopped parsley

grated zest of ½ lemon

1 tsp tomato purée

½ tsp ground mace

2 tomatoes, skinned, seeded and diced

Preparation time: 20 minutes
Cooking time: 20–25 minutes

1 For the blanquette, heat the oil in a flameproof casserole. Add the leeks, onions and bay leaves, stir well and cover. Cook over a gentle heat for 5 minutes or until the leeks are softened slightly and the bay leaves are aromatic.

2 Sprinkle the flour over the leek mixture, then gradually stir in the stock and wine. Halve any large potatoes and add with the mushrooms and chestnuts. Bring to the boil. Reduce the heat, cover and simmer gently for 15–20 minutes, stirring occasionally.

3 Meanwhile, make the chicken liver croutes. Using 1 tbsp of the oil, brush the slices of French bread lightly on both sides. Heat a non-stick frying pan and brown the bread lightly on both sides. (You may have to do this in batches.) Transfer the slices to a baking tray or flameproof dish. Preheat the grill on a low setting.

4 Heat the remaining oil in the pan. Add the shallot and garlic and cook for 2–3 minutes or until softened. Add the bacon and chicken livers and cook for 5 minutes, stirring frequently. Stir in the tarragon, parsley, lemon zest, tomato purée, mace, diced tomatoes and seasoning to taste. Spoon the mixture and any cooking juices onto the bread, pressing it down gently. Turn the grill off and place the croutes in the grill compartment to keep hot.

5 In a small bowl, beat the egg yolk with the cream until thoroughly combined. Stir in 2–3 spoonfuls of the hot cooking liquid from the blanquette, then add the mixture to the pan. Heat gently, stirring, for 30 seconds. Do not allow the sauce to boil or it will curdle. Add the nutmeg, season to taste and remove from the heat.

6 Discard the bay leaves. Ladle the blanquette onto plates or into shallow bowls, garnish with tarragon and serve hot, with the croutes.

Plus points

• Chicken livers are an excellent source of iron. A third of British women under the age of 50 have been shown to have low iron stores, which can lead to tiredness and increased susceptibility to infections.

• Chestnuts are rich in complex carbohydrate and low in fat. They also provide useful amounts of vitamins E and B_6.

special casseroles

Some more ideas

• Cooked chicken or turkey can be added to the blanquette at the end of step 2 – an ideal way to use up leftovers from a roast.

• Sliced fennel and celery are also delicious in the blanquette: add with the leeks and onions. Drained canned artichoke bottoms or hearts can be added for the final 5 minutes of simmering.

• For a vegetarian version, use vegetable stock instead of chicken stock. Top the croutes with a mixture of 55 g (2 oz) crumbled blue cheese, 3 tbsp snipped fresh chives and 4 skinned, seeded and diced tomatoes. Toast under a preheated warm (not too hot) grill for about 2–3 minutes or until the cheese begins to melt.

• Instead of pâté, sprinkle chopped fresh oregano or marjoram and crumbled feta cheese on the croutes.

Each serving provides

kcal 635, **protein** 26 g, **fat** 20 g (of which saturated fat 5 g), **carbohydrate** 86 g (of which sugars 16 g), **fibre** 9 g

✓✓✓	B_2, B_6, B_{12}, C, folate, copper, iron
✓✓	B_1, niacin, phosphorus, potassium, zinc
✓	calcium, selenium

Braised vegetables with falafel and yogurt sauce

As a change from rice, pasta or couscous, try little falafel with a simple vegetable casserole. Made with canned chickpeas and baked rather than deep-fried, these falafel are quick and easy to prepare.

Serves 4

2 tbsp extra virgin olive oil

1 garlic clove, crushed

500 g (1 lb 2 oz) onions, sliced

2 large yellow, red or orange peppers, seeded and sliced

250 g (8½ oz) courgettes

300 ml (10 fl oz) vegetable stock, preferably home-made light or rich (see page 23)

340 g (12 oz) cherry tomatoes, halved

salt and pepper

fresh mint sprigs to garnish

Falafel

2 cans chickpeas, about 400 g each, drained and rinsed

8 spring onions, chopped

6 tbsp chopped parsley

2 tbsp chopped fresh coriander

2 tbsp ground coriander

Yogurt sauce

½ cucumber, grated

85 g (3 oz) watercress leaves, finely shredded

85 g (3 oz) rocket, finely shredded

3 tbsp chopped fresh mint

grated zest of 1 lime

200 g (7 oz) plain low-fat yogurt

Preparation time: 30 minutes

Cooking time: about 1 hour

1 Brush a shallow baking dish or tin with a little oil. Put the chickpeas in a bowl and use a potato masher to mash them, then mix in the spring onions, parsley, fresh and ground coriander, and seasoning to taste. Alternatively, mix the ingredients in a food processor. With your hands, shape the mixture into 24 balls slightly larger than walnuts, placing them in the greased dish or tin. Set aside.

2 Preheat the oven to 200°C (400°F, gas mark 6). Heat the oil in a flameproof casserole. Add the garlic, onions and peppers. Stir well, then cover and cook gently, stirring frequently, for 15 minutes or until the vegetables are soft but not browned.

3 Stir in the courgettes and stock. Bring to the boil, then cover the casserole and transfer it to the oven. Place the falafel in the oven at the same time. Cook for 20 minutes.

4 Add the tomatoes to the casserole and stir. Cover and return it to the oven. Use a spoon and fork to turn the falafel, taking care not to break them. Cook the casserole and falafel for a further 20 minutes or until the vegetables are tender and the falafel are crisp and lightly browned.

5 Meanwhile, to make the yogurt sauce, squeeze the cucumber in handfuls to remove excess moisture. Put it into a bowl. Stir in the watercress, rocket, mint, lime zest and yogurt. Add seasoning to taste and transfer to a serving dish. Cover and chill until ready to serve.

6 Transfer the falafel to a serving dish. Taste the casserole for seasoning, garnish with mint sprigs and serve with the falafel and yogurt sauce.

Plus points

• Chickpeas are a good source of dietary fibre, particularly the soluble fibre that can help reduce high blood cholesterol levels.

• Watercress has been considered something of a superfood for many centuries. Hippocrates wrote about its medicinal values in 460 BC and built the world's first hospital next to a stream so he could grow fresh watercress. Watercress provides good amounts of several antioxidants, including vitamins C and E, and carotenoid compounds. It also contributes substantial amounts of folate, niacin and vitamin B_6.

Each serving provides ⓥ

kcal 400, **protein** 21 g, **fat** 12 g (of which
saturated fat 2 g), **carbohydrate** 53 g (of
which sugars 24 g), **fibre** 13 g

✓✓✓	A, B₆, C, E, iron
✓✓	folate, calcium, phosphorus, zinc
✓	B₁, niacin, potassium

Some more ideas

• The vegetable casserole and falafel are both
good cold as well as hot. Stir a little chopped
fresh mint and parsley into the casserole just
before serving.

• To turn the casserole into a ratatouille, use
250 g (8½ oz) onions and add 1 diced
aubergine with the courgettes. Replace the

cherry tomatoes with 500 g (1 lb 2 oz) skinned
and quartered plum tomatoes.

• Garlic lovers will enjoy additional garlic in the
falafel – add 2 crushed garlic cloves and the
grated zest of 1 lemon for a punchy flavour.

• Basil is splendid in the yogurt sauce – shred
a handful of fresh leaves and add them with or
instead of the rocket.

A glossary of nutritional terms

Antioxidants These are compounds that help to protect the body's cells against the damaging effects of free radicals. Vitamins C and E, beta-carotene (the plant form of vitamin A) and the mineral selenium, together with many of the phytochemicals found in fruit and vegetables, all act as antioxidants.

Calorie A unit used to measure the energy value of food and the intake and use of energy by the body. The scientific definition of 1 calorie is the amount of heat required to raise the temperature of 1 gram of water by 1 degree Centigrade. This is such a small amount that in this country we tend to use the term kilocalories (abbreviated to *kcal*), which is equivalent to 1000 calories. Energy values can also be measured in kilojoules (kJ): 1 kcal = 4.2 kJ.

A person's energy (calorie) requirement varies depending on his or her age, sex and level of activity. The estimated average daily energy requirements are:

Age (years)	Female (kcal)	Male (kcal)
1–3	1165	1230
4–6	1545	1715
7–10	1740	1970
11–14	1845	2220
15–18	2110	2755
19–49	1940	2550
50–59	1900	2550
60–64	1900	2380
65–74	1900	2330

Carbohydrates These energy-providing substances are present in varying amounts in different foods and are found in three main forms: sugars, starches and non-starch polysaccharides (NSP), usually called fibre.

There are two types of sugars: *intrinsic sugars*, which occur naturally in fruit (fructose) and sweet-tasting vegetables, and *extrinsic sugars*, which include lactose (from milk) and all the non-milk extrinsic sugars (NMEs) – sucrose (table sugar), honey, treacle, molasses and so on. The NMEs, or 'added' sugars, provide only calories, whereas foods containing intrinsic sugars also offer vitamins, minerals and fibre. Added sugars (*simple carbohydrates*) are digested and absorbed rapidly to provide energy very quickly. Starches and fibre (*complex carbohydrates*), on the other hand, break down more slowly to offer a longer-term energy source (see also Glycaemic Index). Starchy carbohydrates are found in bread, pasta, rice,

wholegrain and breakfast cereals, and potatoes and other starchy vegetables such as parsnips, sweet potatoes and yams.

Healthy eating guidelines recommend that at least half of our daily energy (calories) should come from carbohydrates, and that most of this should be from complex carbohydrates. No more than 11% of our total calorie intake should come from 'added' sugars. For an average woman aged 19–49 years, this would mean a total carbohydrate intake of 259 g per day, of which 202 g should be from starch and intrinsic sugars and no more than 57 g from added sugars. For a man of the same age, total carbohydrates each day should be about 340 g (265 g from starch and intrinsic sugars and 75 g from added sugars).

See also Fibre and Glycogen.

Cholesterol There are two types of cholesterol – the soft waxy substance called blood cholesterol, which is an integral part of human cell membranes, and dietary cholesterol, which is contained in food. *Blood cholesterol* is important in the formation of some hormones and it aids digestion. High blood cholesterol levels are known to be an important risk factor for coronary heart disease, but most of the cholesterol in our blood is made by the liver – only about 25% comes from cholesterol in food. So while it would seem that the amount of cholesterol-rich foods in the diet would have a direct effect on blood cholesterol levels, in fact the best way to reduce blood cholesterol is to eat less saturated fat and to increase intake of foods containing soluble fibre.

Fat Although a small amount of fat is essential for good health, most people consume far too much. Healthy eating guidelines recommend that no more than 33% of our daily energy intake (calories) should come from fat. Each gram of fat contains 9 kcal, more than twice as many calories as carbohydrate or protein, so for a woman aged 19–49 years this means a daily maximum of 71 g fat, and for a man in the same age range 93.5 g fat.

Fats can be divided into 3 main groups: saturated, monounsaturated and polyunsaturated, depending on the chemical structure of the fatty acids they contain. *Saturated fatty acids* are found mainly in animal fats such as butter and other dairy products and in fatty meat. A high intake of saturated fat is known to be a risk factor for coronary heart disease and certain types of cancer. Current guidelines are that no more than 10% of our daily calories should come from saturated fats, which is about 21.5 g for an adult woman and 28.5 g for a man.

Where saturated fats tend to be solid at room temperature, the *unsaturated fatty acids* –

monounsaturated and polyunsaturated – tend to be liquid. *Monounsaturated fats* are found predominantly in olive oil, groundnut (peanut) oil, rapeseed oil and avocados. Foods high in *polyunsaturates* include most vegetable oils – the exceptions are palm oil and coconut oil, both of which are saturated.

Both saturated and monounsaturated fatty acids can be made by the body, but certain polyunsaturated fatty acids – known as *essential fatty acids* – must be supplied by food. There are 2 'families' of these essential fatty acids: *omega-6*, derived from linoleic acid, and *omega-3*, from linolenic acid. The main food sources of the omega-6 family are vegetable oils such as olive and sunflower; omega-3 fatty acids are provided by oily fish, nuts, and vegetable oils such as soya and rapeseed.

When vegetable oils are hydrogenated (hardened) to make margarine and reduced-fat spreads, their unsaturated fatty acids can be changed into trans fatty acids, or '*trans fats*'. These artificially produced trans fats are believed to act in the same way as saturated fats within the body – with the same risks to health. Current healthy eating guidelines suggest that no more than 2% of our daily calories should come from trans fats, which is about 4.3 g for an adult woman and 5.6 g for a man. In thinking about the amount of trans fats you consume, remember that major sources are processed foods such as biscuits, pies, cakes and crisps.

Fibre Technically non-starch polysaccharides (NSP), fibre is the term commonly used to describe several different compounds, such as pectin, hemicellulose, lignin and gums, which are found in the cell walls of all plants. The body cannot digest fibre, nor does it have much nutritional value, but it plays an important role in helping us to stay healthy.

Fibre can be divided into 2 groups – soluble and insoluble. Both types are provided by most plant foods, but some foods are particularly good sources of one type or the other. *Soluble fibre* (in oats, pulses, fruit and vegetables) can help to reduce high blood cholesterol levels and to control blood sugar levels by slowing down the absorption of sugar. *Insoluble fibre* (in wholegrain cereals, pulses, fruit and vegetables) increases stool bulk and speeds the passage of waste material through the body. In this way it helps to prevent constipation, haemorrhoids and diverticular disease, and may protect against bowel cancer.

Our current intake of fibre is around 12 g a day. Healthy eating guidelines suggest that we need to increase this amount to 18 g a day.

Free radicals These highly reactive molecules can cause damage to cell walls and DNA (the genetic material found within cells). They are believed to be involved in the development of heart disease, some cancers and premature ageing. Free radicals are produced naturally by the body in the course of everyday life, but certain factors, such as cigarette smoke, pollution and over-exposure to sunlight, can accelerate their production.

Gluten A protein found in wheat and, to a lesser degree, in rye, barley and oats, but not in corn (maize) or rice. People with *coeliac disease* have a sensitivity to gluten and need to eliminate all gluten-containing foods, such as bread, pasta, cakes and biscuits, from their diet.

Glycaemic Index (GI) This is used to measure the rate at which carbohydrate foods are digested and converted into sugar (glucose) to raise blood sugar levels and provide energy. Foods with a high GI are quickly broken down and offer an immediate energy fix, while those with a lower GI are absorbed more slowly, making you feel full for longer and helping to keep blood sugar levels constant. High-GI foods include table sugar, honey, mashed potatoes and watermelon. Low-GI foods include pulses, wholewheat cereals, apples, cherries, dried apricots, pasta and oats.

Glycogen This is one of the 2 forms in which energy from carbohydrates is made available for use by the body (the other is *glucose*). Whereas glucose is converted quickly from carbohydrates and made available in the blood for a fast energy fix, glycogen is stored in the liver and muscles to fuel longer-term energy needs. When the body has used up its immediate supply of glucose, the stored glycogen is broken down into glucose to continue supplying energy.

Minerals These inorganic substances perform a wide range of vital functions in the body. The *macrominerals* – calcium, chloride, magnesium, potassium, phosphorus and sodium – are needed in relatively large quantities, whereas much smaller amounts are required of the remainder, called *microminerals*. Some microminerals (selenium, magnesium and iodine, for example) are needed in such tiny amounts that they are known as *'trace elements'*.

There are important differences in the body's ability to absorb minerals from different foods, and this can be affected by the presence of other substances. For example, oxalic acid, present in spinach, interferes with the absorption of much of the iron and calcium spinach contains.
• *Calcium* is essential for the development of strong bones and teeth. It also plays an important role in blood clotting. Good sources include dairy products, canned fish (eaten with their bones) and dark green, leafy vegetables.
• *Chloride* helps to maintain the body's fluid balance. The main source in the diet is table salt.
• *Chromium* is important in the regulation of blood sugar levels, as well as levels of fat and cholesterol in the blood. Good dietary sources include red meat, liver, eggs, seafood, cheese and wholegrain cereals.

• *Copper*, component of many enzymes, is needed for bone growth and the formation of connective tissue. It helps the body to absorb iron from food. Good sources include offal, shellfish, mushrooms, cocoa, nuts and seeds.
• *Iodine* is an important component of the thyroid hormones, which govern the rate and efficiency at which food is converted into energy. Good sources include seafood, seaweed and vegetables (depending on the iodine content of the soil in which they are grown).
• *Iron* is an essential component of haemoglobin, the pigment in red blood cells that carries oxygen around the body. Good sources are offal, red meat, dried apricots and prunes, and iron-fortified breakfast cereals.
• *Magnesium* is important for healthy bones, the release of energy from food, and nerve and muscle function. Good sources include wholegrain cereals, peas and other green vegetables, pulses, dried fruit and nuts.
• *Manganese* is a vital component of several enzymes that are involved in energy production and many other functions. Good dietary sources include nuts, cereals, brown rice, pulses and wholemeal bread.
• *Molybdenum* is an essential component of several enzymes, including those involved in the production of DNA. Good sources are offal, yeast, pulses, wholegrain cereals and green leafy vegetables.
• *Phosphorus* is important for healthy bones and teeth and for the release of energy from foods. It is found in most foods. Particularly good sources include dairy products, red meat, poultry, fish and eggs.
• *Potassium*, along with sodium, is important in maintaining fluid balance and regulating blood pressure, and is essential for the transmission of nerve impulses. Good sources include fruit, especially bananas and citrus fruits, nuts, seeds, potatoes and pulses.
• *Selenium* is a powerful antioxidant that protects cells against damage by free radicals. Good dietary sources are meat, fish, dairy foods, brazil nuts, avocados and lentils.
• *Sodium* works with potassium to regulate fluid balance, and is essential for nerve and muscle function. Only a little sodium is needed – we tend to get too much in our diet. The main source in the diet is table salt, as well as salty processed foods and ready-prepared foods.
• *Sulphur* is a component of 2 essential amino acids. Protein foods are the main source.
• *Zinc* is vital for normal growth, as well as reproduction and immunity. Good dietary sources include oysters, red meat, peanuts and sunflower seeds.

Phytochemicals These biologically active compounds, found in most plant foods, are believed to be beneficial in disease prevention. There are literally thousands of different phytochemicals, amongst which are the following:

• *Allicin*, a phytochemical found in garlic, onions, leeks, chives and shallots, is believed to help lower high blood cholesterol levels and stimulate the immune system.
• *Bioflavonoids*, of which there are at least 6000, are found mainly in fruit and sweet-tasting vegetables. Different bioflavonoids have different roles – some are antioxidants, while others act as anti-disease agents. A sub-group of these phytochemicals, called *flavonols*, includes the antioxidant *quercetin*, which is believed to reduce the risk of heart disease and help to protect against cataracts. Quercetin is found in tea, red wine, grapes and broad beans.
• *Carotenoids*, the best known of which are *beta-carotene* and *lycopene*, are powerful antioxidants thought to help protect us against certain types of cancer. Highly coloured fruits and vegetables, such as blackcurrants, mangoes, tomatoes, carrots, sweet potatoes, pumpkin and dark green, leafy vegetables, are excellent sources of carotenoids.
• *Coumarins* are believed to help protect against cancer by inhibiting the formation of tumours. Oranges are a rich source.
• *Glucosinolates*, found mainly in cruciferous vegetables, particularly broccoli, Brussels sprouts, cabbage, kale and cauliflower, are believed to have strong anti-cancer effects. *Sulphoraphane* is one of the powerful cancer-fighting substances produced by glucosinolates.
• *Phytoestrogens* have a chemical structure similar to the female hormone oestrogen, and they are believed to help protect against hormone-related cancers such as breast and prostate cancer. One of the types of these phytochemicals, called *isoflavones*, may also help to relieve symptoms associated with the menopause. Soya beans and chickpeas are a particularly rich source of isoflavones.

Protein This nutrient, necessary for growth and development, for maintenance and repair of cells, and for the production of enzymes, antibodies and hormones, is essential to keep the body working efficiently. Protein is made up of *amino acids*, which are compounds containing the 4 elements that are necessary for life: carbon, hydrogen, oxygen and nitrogen. We need all of the 20 amino acids commonly found in plant and animal proteins. The human body can make 12 of these, but the remaining 8 – called *essential amino acids* – must be obtained from the food we eat.

Protein comes in a wide variety of foods. Meat, fish, dairy products, eggs and soya beans contain all of the essential amino acids, and are therefore called first-class protein foods. Pulses, nuts, seeds and cereals are also good sources of protein, but do not contain the full range of essential amino acids. In practical terms, this really doesn't matter – as long as you include a variety of different protein foods in your diet, your body will get all the amino acids it needs. It is important, though, to eat protein foods every day because the essential amino acids cannot be stored in the body for later use.

The RNI of protein for women aged 19–49 years is 45 g per day and for men of the same age 55 g. In the UK most people eat more protein than they need, although this isn't normally a problem.

Reference Nutrient Intake (RNI)
This denotes the average daily amount of vitamins and minerals thought to be sufficient to meet the nutritional needs of almost all individuals within the population. The figures, published by the Department of Health, vary depending on age, sex and specific nutritional needs such as pregnancy. RNIs are equivalent to what used to be called Recommended Daily Amounts or Allowances (RDA).

RNIs for adults (19–49 years)

Vitamin A	600–700 mcg
Vitamin B_1	0.8 mg for women, 1 mg for men
Vitamin B_2	1.1 mg for women, 1.3 mg for men
Niacin	13 mg for women, 17 mg for men
Vitamin B_6	1.2 mg for women, 1.4 mg for men
Vitamin B_{12}	1.5 mg
Folate	200 mcg (400 mcg for first trimester of pregnancy)
Vitamin C	40 mg
Vitamin E	no recommendation in the UK; the EC RDA is 10 mg, which has been used in all recipe analyses in this book
Calcium	700 mg
Chloride	2500 mg
Copper	1.2 mg
Iodine	140 mcg
Iron	14.8 mg for women, 8.7 mg for men
Magnesium	270–300 mg
Phosphorus	550 mg
Potassium	3500 mg
Selenium	60 mcg for women, 75 mcg for men
Sodium	1600 mg
Zinc	7 mg for women, 9.5 mg for men

Vitamins These are organic compounds that are essential for good health. Although they are required in only small amounts, each one has specific vital functions to perform. Most vitamins cannot be made by the human body, and therefore must be obtained from the diet. The body is capable of storing some vitamins (A, D, E, K and B_{12}), but the rest need to be provided by the diet on a regular basis. A well-balanced diet, containing a wide variety of different foods, is the best way to ensure that you get all the vitamins you need.

Vitamins can be divided into 2 groups: *water-soluble* (B complex and C) and *fat-soluble* (A, D, E and K). Water-soluble vitamins are easily destroyed during processing, storage, and the preparation and cooking of food. The fat-soluble vitamins are less vulnerable to losses during cooking and processing.

• *Vitamin A* (retinol) is essential for healthy vision, eyes, skin and growth. Good sources include dairy products, offal (especially liver), eggs and oily fish. Vitamin A can also be obtained from *beta-carotene*, the pigment found in highly coloured fruit and vegetables. In addition to acting as a source of vitamin A, beta-carotene has an important role to play as an antioxidant in its own right.

• *The B Complex vitamins* have very similar roles to play in nutrition, and many of them occur together in the same foods.
Vitamin B_1 (thiamin) is essential in the release of energy from carbohydrates. Good sources include milk, offal, meat (especially pork), wholegrain and fortified breakfast cereals, nuts and pulses, yeast extract and wheat germ. White flour and bread are fortified with B_1 in the UK.
Vitamin B_2 (riboflavin) is vital for growth, healthy skin and eyes, and the release of energy from food. Good sources include milk, meat, offal, eggs, cheese, fortified breakfast cereals, yeast extract and green leafy vegetables.
Niacin (nicotinic acid), sometimes called vitamin B_3, plays an important role in the release of energy within the cells. Unlike the other B vitamins it can be made by the body from the essential amino acid tryptophan. Good sources include meat, offal, fish, fortified breakfast cereals and pulses. White flour and bread are fortified with niacin in the UK.
Pantothenic acid, sometimes called vitamin B_5, is involved in a number of metabolic reactions, including energy production. This vitamin is present in most foods; notable exceptions are fat, oil and sugar. Good sources include liver, kidneys, yeast, egg yolks, fish roe, wheat germ, nuts, pulses and fresh vegetables.
Vitamin B_6 (pyridoxine) helps the body to utilise protein and contributes to the formation of haemoglobin for red blood cells. B_6 is found in a wide range of foods including meat, liver, fish, eggs, wholegrain cereals, some vegetables, pulses, brown rice, nuts and yeast extract.
Vitamin B_{12} (cyanocobalamin) is vital for growth, the formation of red blood cells and maintenance of a healthy nervous system. B_{12} is unique in that it is principally found in foods of animal origin. Vegetarians who eat dairy products will get enough, but vegans need to ensure they include food fortified with B_{12} in their diet. Good sources of B_{12} include liver, kidneys, oily fish, meat, cheese, eggs and milk.
Folate (folic acid) is involved in the manufacture of amino acids and in the production of red blood cells. Recent research suggests that folate may also help to protect against heart disease. Good sources of folate are green leafy vegetables, liver, pulses, eggs, wholegrain cereal products and fortified breakfast cereals, brewers' yeast, wheatgerm, nuts and fruit, especially grapefruit and oranges.
Biotin is needed for various metabolic reactions and the release of energy from foods. Good sources include liver, oily fish, brewers' yeast, kidneys, egg yolks and brown rice.

• *Vitamin C* (ascorbic acid) is essential for growth and vital for the formation of collagen (a protein needed for healthy bones, teeth, gums, blood capillaries and all connective tissue). It plays an important role in the healing of wounds and fractures, and acts as a powerful antioxidant. Vitamin C is found mainly in fruit and vegetables.

• *Vitamin D* (cholecalciferol) is essential for growth and the absorption of calcium, and thus for the formation of healthy bones. It is also involved in maintaining a healthy nervous system. The amount of vitamin D occurring naturally in foods is small, and it is found in very few foods – good sources are oily fish (and fish liver oil supplements), eggs and liver, as well as breakfast cereals, margarine and full-fat milk that are fortified with vitamin D. Most vitamin D, however, does not come from the diet but is made by the body when the skin is exposed to sunlight.

• *Vitamin E* is not one vitamin, but a number of related compounds called tocopherols that function as antioxidants. Good sources of vitamin E are vegetable oils, polyunsaturated margarines, wheatgerm, sunflower seeds, nuts, oily fish, eggs, wholegrain cereals, avocados and spinach.

• *Vitamin K* is essential for the production of several proteins, including prothombin which is involved in the clotting of blood. It has been found to exist in 3 forms, one of which is obtained from food while the other 2 are made by the bacteria in the intestine. Vitamin K_1, which is the form found in food, is present in broccoli, cabbage, spinach, milk, margarine, vegetable oils, particularly soya oil, cereals, liver, alfalfa and kelp.

Nutritional analyses
The nutritional analysis of each recipe has been carried out using data from *The Composition of Foods* with additional data from food manufacturers where appropriate. Because the level and availability of different nutrients can vary, depending on factors like growing conditions and breed of animal, the figures are intended as an approximate guide only.

The analyses include vitamins A, B_1, B_2, B_6, B_{12}, niacin, folate, C, D and E, and the minerals calcium, copper, iron, potassium, selenium and zinc. Other vitamins and minerals are not included, as deficiencies are rare. Optional ingredients and optional serving suggestions have not been included in the calculations.

Index

*Printing and binding: Tien Wah
Press Limited, Singapore
Separations: Colour Systems Ltd,
London
Paper: StoraEnso*

index